PrimeFaces Theme Development

Create, package, and customize stunning themes using PrimeFaces

Andy Bailey

Sudheer Jonna

BIRMINGHAM - MUMBAI

PrimeFaces Theme Development

First published: October 2015

Production reference: 1231015

Published by Packt Publishing Ltd.
Livery Place
35 Livery Street
Birmingham B3 2PB, UK.

ISBN 978-1-78398-868-6

www.packtpub.com

Credits

Authors
Andy Bailey
Sudheer Jonna

Reviewers
Aristides Villarreal Bravo
Sebastian D'Agostino
Daswanth Karuchola
Glauco Márdano
Daryl Mathison

Commissioning Editor
Amarabha Banerjee

Acquisition Editor
Usha Iyer

Content Development Editor
Arun Nadar

Technical Editor
Gaurav Suri

Copy Editor
Vedangi Narvekar

Project Coordinator
Neha Bhatnagar

Proofreader
Safis Editing

Indexer
Hemangini Bari

Graphics
Abhinash Sahu

Production Coordinator
Nitesh Thakur

Cover Work
Nitesh Thakur

About the Authors

Andy Bailey is a middle-aged Java enthusiast. He has been involved in Java development since the humble beginnings of Java 1.0.1 in 1995. He thoroughly enjoys challenges even more so now than ever.

He has had a varied career, including extended employment with the UK Ministry of Defence, youth outreach programs as a volunteer, and a volunteer paramedic.

After gaining a degree in computer science with artificial intelligence from the University of Sussex, he immigrated to Germany in 1996. He learned how to speak and write in German while being involved in projects as diverse as 24/7 multimedia live streaming and buffering free multimedia playback to design, develop, and build systems to control, monitor, and analyze data collected from gaming machines in a widely distributed environment.

This is his first publication. However, he has helped review other publications, including *PrimeFaces Cookbook*.

To my wife, Monika, all my family, friends and colleagues I give a big thank you for giving me the time to write this book.

To the Packt Team and especially Sudheer; without you this would not have been possible. Words cannot begin to express my thanks.

Sudheer Jonna was born in Andhra Pradesh, India, in 1987. Currently, he works as a senior software engineer in Chennai, India. He completed his master's degree in computer applications from JNTU. In the past 4-5 years, he worked on providing architectural designs and building various web applications based on JSF, Struts, Spring, jQuery, JPA, EJB, and various Java EE and frontend technologies.

He is a JSF and PrimeFaces expert. He has been working with the PrimeFaces component library since 2011. He worked as a committer and project member of PrimeFaces and PrimeFaces Extensions open source projects. He has been a well-known, recognized member of the PrimeFaces community for the past few years. He is also the author of *Learning PrimeFaces Extensions Development* and *PrimeFaces BluePrints* books, *Packt Publishing*. He worked as reviewer for *PrimeFaces Beginner's Guide* and community reviewer for many other books.

Besides working with the aforementioned technologies, he also writes technical articles, provides online training, designs and develops web application architecture, writes books and reviews, and provides suggestions through online forums and blogs. He is interested in the research and development of various popular Java EE frameworks and many other latest technologies.

He shares his knowledge through GitHub (https://github.com/sudheerj). He recently started blogging (http://sudheerjonna.blogspot.in/). You can follow him on Twitter (@SudheerJonna) or contact him on Gmail at sudheer.jonna@gmail.com.

I would like to thank my co-author, Andy Bailey, the PrimeFaces lead, Cagatay Civici, the Packt book reviewers, and the Packt team for their support and great teamwork in the past few years.

Also, a huge thanks to my family members, colleagues, and friends for their support in completing this book in a short span of time.

About the Reviewers

Aristides Villarreal Bravo is a Java developer and a member of the NetBeans Dream Team and Java User Groups Leaders. He lives in Panama.

He has organized and participated in various national and international conferences and seminars related to Java, Java EE, NetBeans, NetBeans platform, free software, and mobile devices.

He writes tutorials and blogs about Java, NetBeans, and web developers. He has reviewed several books for Packt Publishing. He also develops plugins for NetBeans.

He specializes in JSE, JEE, JPA, Agile, and Continuous Integration. He shares his knowledge via his blog, which can be viewed at `http://avbravo.blogspot.com`. He is the CEO of JavScAz Software Developers.

To my family.

Sebastian D'Agostino lives in Argentina. He earned his computer software engineer degree from the University of Buenos Aires (UBA). He has been developing with C, C++, and Java EE in a professional manner for 6 years. He worked for big multinational companies such as Oracle as well as participated in freelance work. He was involved in different projects pertaining to backend, middleware, frontend and even functional analysis. His frontend experience includes Struts, PrimeFaces, and AngularJS. Presently, he is working for Banco Industrial (Bind, Industrial Bank) and studying for master's in information technology and communications at Universidad Argentina de la Empresa (UADE).

I would like to thank my parents and my family for their constant support towards my decisions related to my life and career.

Daswanth Karuchola is currently working as a software developer with more than 8 years of relevant background in software development. He has knowledge of software development processes (such as Agile and Scrum) and practices (such as TDD), functional and object-oriented paradigms, the Java, C++, and C# programming languages, Java EE, and the Windows and Linux operating systems.

He is highly proficient in Java, JSF, PrimeFaces, and RichFaces. He would like to dabble in Hadoop and Cloud computing.

He has experience working with Java EE 1.4+ (JPA/JTA/JAXB/JSF/JSP/JDBC/JNDI/JMS/JAX-WS/JAX-RS/Servlets/Spring/Hibernate/Apache ActiveMQ/Apache CXF/Apache Lucene/Apache HBase/Infinispan/EhCache/Hazelcast/Websockets), MySQL, PostgreSQL, Eclipse, C++ Builder, MongoDB, Redis, and Oracle.

He specializes in software development, distributed systems, web applications, desktop application, rich Internet applications (RIA), cloud computing, databases, and NoSQL solutions.

Glauco Márdano is 24, has a degree in system analysis, and has been working with Java web development for about 3 years. His main interests are related to technology and finance. He likes to learn new subjects pertaining to his interests.

He is also the author of *jMonkeyEngine 3.0 Cookbook*, *Learning Pentesting for Android Devices*, and *Learning Android Intents* from Packt Publishing.

I'd like to thank Neha Bhatnagar for being very patient with the reviewing process. She's done a great job with the project management, and I'm very pleased about it.

Daryl Mathison has been heavily involved in computers since he was in elementary school. He has been professionally developing software since 1998. He has used C, C++, Java, and Python to solve various software problems. He writes a blog about Java, which has been reposted in Java Coding Geeks several times. The subjects that he is current exploring are OSGi, Maven, and cloud computing.

I would like to acknowledge my wonderful wife. She has been patient and understanding through the nights that were taken up by the reviewing of this book.

www.PacktPub.com

Support files, eBooks, discount offers, and more

For support files and downloads related to your book, please visit www.PacktPub.com.

Did you know that Packt offers eBook versions of every book published, with PDF and ePub files available? You can upgrade to the eBook version at www.PacktPub.com and as a print book customer, you are entitled to a discount on the eBook copy. Get in touch with us at service@packtpub.com for more details.

At www.PacktPub.com, you can also read a collection of free technical articles, sign up for a range of free newsletters and receive exclusive discounts and offers on Packt books and eBooks.

https://www2.packtpub.com/books/subscription/packtlib

Do you need instant solutions to your IT questions? PacktLib is Packt's online digital book library. Here, you can search, access, and read Packt's entire library of books.

Why subscribe?

- Fully searchable across every book published by Packt
- Copy and paste, print, and bookmark content
- On demand and accessible via a web browser

Free access for Packt account holders

If you have an account with Packt at www.PacktPub.com, you can use this to access PacktLib today and view 9 entirely free books. Simply use your login credentials for immediate access.

Table of Contents

Preface

One of the most popular and commonly used web application frameworks today is JavaServer Faces (JSF) 2.2. Since the introduction of JSF 2, there are a plethora of component libraries that provide more functionality than that provided by standard JSF components. PrimeFaces is one of the leading component libraries available today.

PrimeFaces not only provides a rich set of UI components, but also has the concept of themes integrated from the beginning. PrimeFaces themes use jQuery UI as a foundation, which makes adapting to the existing or creating completely customized themes a gentle and rewarding process. Because jQuery UI is used to create themes, there is a plethora of documentation and tools available for you to use. This makes working with PrimeFaces themes very easy.

This book is aimed at the developers of Java Server Faces web applications; these applications use the PrimeFaces component library. Together, we are going to have a look at how to use built-in PrimeFaces themes, adjust these themes to fit a particular application's needs, and finally create custom themes for both desktop- and mobile-based web apps. By the time you have read this book and worked on the examples provided in its chapters, you will hopefully have gained valuable insights into the PrimeFaces technology, and especially into how PrimeFaces themes can be used to enrich user experience for your applications.

The practical exercises in the book can be run using any web server that supports JSF2/2.2 and Java 6+. The IDE used for the examples in the book was NetBeans 8.0.1, but any IDE that supports Maven and a suitable web/application server can be used in its place.

What this book covers

Chapter 1, To Skin an App, covers how to create a JSF project and integrate the PrimeFaces library into it. The chapter is meant to bring all the readers onto a level playing field and provide a platform from which both the book and a PrimeFaces theme can be built.

Chapter 2, Introducing PrimeFaces Themes, compares the standard JSF and PrimeFaces components and highlights that JSF does not provide for theming by itself, but it does provide mechanisms to extend the capabilities of the framework to include themes and a rich set of components.

Chapter 3, jQuery UI, ThemeRoller, and the Anatomy of a Theme, explains how at theme is structured and how PrimeFaces uses jQuery UI to apply a theme to your application.

Chapter 4, A PrimeFaces inputText Component in Detail, takes a simple UI component and uses browser developer tools to examine and change the CSS rules applied to it. In this chapter, we will strip away some of the mysteries involved in applying a Theme to your application.

Chapter 5, Let's Get Creative, builds on the work in the previous chapter by using a custom theme and tweaking it according to our needs. This will expose some of the weaknesses of ThemeRoller-generated themes and how to compensate for them.

Chapter 6, Icons, explains the role of icons in the PrimeFaces web application by using icons from the standard theme icon set, creating custom icons, and applying them on some PrimeFaces components for demonstration purposes. This chapter also introduces the Font Awesome icons apart from the regular ThemeRoller icons.

Chapter 7, Dynamic Changes – a Working Example, explores how to use a combination of JavaScript and CSS to enhance an application. Themes can only do so much and quite often, we want to enhance the way a PrimeFaces component looks like depending on the state of the underlying data.

Chapter 8, Mobile Web Apps, talks about PrimeFaces Mobile and how to create customized mobile themes using ThemeRoller and apply a customized mobile theme that is suitable for mobile web applications.

Chapter 9, The Final Touches, explains how to make sure that the newly created desktop/mobile theme is complete by applying it to the PrimeFaces showcase application and performing the common component-specific CSS modifications to finalize the theme JAR files according to users' interests.

Chapter 10, Theme Design Best Practices, looks at best practices in theme development. We will also look at generally applicable best practices in web design as well as those for rich Internet applications and PrimeFaces themes.

Chapter 11, Premium Themes and Layouts, and Third-party Converter Tools, explores the usage of premium themes and layouts and how modern technologies such as LESS CSS Preprocessor, the Google Material Design language, and so on, introduced in them to provide amazing templates. This chapter also introduces third-party theme converter tools that are available in the market.

What you need for this book

As a JSF developer, you should already have in-depth knowledge of general Java programming, JSF and/or Java EE 6 or 7, (X)HTML, CSS, and JavaScript. In addition to this, a familiarity with the PrimeFaces component library will be of help when reading and working through the examples in the book. A working knowledge of Maven will also be of help.

The following are the additional requirements for this book:

- Recommended JSF: Java 7
- Recommended IDE: NetBeans 8
- Recommended web server: Glassfish 4
- The PrimeFaces version being used is freely available PrimeFaces 5.2
- A fork of the Git-based Project accompanies this book

If you already have ideas for a custom theme, then you will have an even more enjoyable time in the later chapters.

The most important thing that you will need is a desire to be creative when designing web applications. A well-thought-out look and feel of an application is what gives your users the best first impression. These impressions are the ones that are the strongest and most lasting.

You will need the following additional resources as well:

- PrimeFaces website
- jQuery and jQuery UI
- CSS reference

Because we don't want to enter the debate about which browser is the best and why others shouldn't be used, the choice of browser is up to you. I prefer using Google Chrome because of its developer tools as well as for more mundane reasons. The only requirement is that it supports CSS3, HTML5, and JavaScript and has a tool for the examination and changing of DOM elements on the fly. The screenshots in this book will show me using Google Chrome.

Who this book is for

This book is for the following two main audiences:

- Web designers who need or are interested in an introduction to PrimeFaces, with an emphasis on theme development

- JSF/Java EE developers who are mainly responsible for middle and backend component development but who either need to know more about the UI, especially using PrimeFaces, or who are keen to expand their knowledge of how it all works.

The book is also aimed at anyone who is interested in JSF because with JSF, it is easy for non-UI specialists to create user interfaces and with PrimeFaces, it is easy to build them with a good look and feel from the word go. The book explains how PrimeFaces themes work and, more importantly, provides insights into how to create custom themes.

Conventions

In this book, you will find a number of styles of text that distinguish between different kinds of information. Here are some examples of these styles, and an explanation of their meaning.

Code words in text, database table names, folder names, filenames, file extensions, pathnames, dummy URLs, user input, and Twitter handles are shown as follows: "Fortunately, the schedule component provides a simple client-side API, which includes the `update()` method to save the bandwidth and increase the page load performance."

A block of code is set as follows:

```
<h:form id="mainform">
  <h:panelGrid id="maintable" columns="2">
    <h:outputLabel id="simpleLabel1" value="A standard inputText
      component:" for="standardInput"/>
    <h:inputText id="standardInput"/>
    <p:outputLabel id="pfLabel2" value="A PrimeFaces inputText
      component:" for="pfInput"/>
    <p:inputText id="pfInput"/>
  </h:panelGrid>
</h:form>
```

When we wish to draw your attention to a particular part of a code block, the relevant lines or items are set in bold:

```
<p:submenu id="chapter2" label="Chapter 2">
  <p:menuitem id="c2difference" value="Differences"
    url="/chapter2/difference.xhtml"/>
  <p:menuitem id="c2morecomponents" value="Mini Showcase"
    url="/chapter2/morecomponents.xhtml"/>
</p:submenu>
```

Any command-line input or output is written as follows:

```
git clone https://github.com/primefaces/showcase.git
```

New terms and **important words** are shown in bold. Words that you see on the screen, in menus or dialog boxes for example, appear in the text like this: "Choose the file or drag and drop the ThemeRoller theme in the ZIP format and click on the **create theme jar** button."

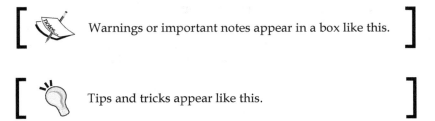

Warnings or important notes appear in a box like this.

Tips and tricks appear like this.

Reader feedback

Feedback from our readers is always welcome. Let us know what you think about this book—what you liked or may have disliked. Reader feedback is important for us to develop titles that you really get the most out of.

To send us general feedback, simply send an e-mail to feedback@packtpub.com, and mention the book title via the subject of your message.

If there is a topic that you have expertise in and you are interested in either writing or contributing to a book, see our author guide on www.packtpub.com/authors.

Customer support

Now that you are the proud owner of a Packt book, we have a number of things to help you to get the most from your purchase.

Downloading the example code

You can download the example code files for all Packt books you have purchased from your account at http://www.packtpub.com. If you purchased this book elsewhere, you can visit http://www.packtpub.com/support and register to have the files e-mailed directly to you.

All the projects or source code for this book are available in the GitHub repository. You can download it from the following link: https://github.com/andyba/PFThemes

Downloading the color images of this book

We also provide you a PDF file that has color images of the screenshots/diagrams used in this book. The color images will help you better understand the changes in the output. You can download this file from: https://www.packtpub.com/sites/default/files/downloads/8686OS_ColoredImages.pdf.

Errata

Although we have taken every care to ensure the accuracy of our content, mistakes do happen. If you find a mistake in one of our books—maybe a mistake in the text or the code—we would be grateful if you would report this to us. By doing so, you can save other readers from frustration and help us improve subsequent versions of this book. If you find any errata, please report them by visiting http://www.packtpub.com/submit-errata, selecting your book, clicking on the **errata submission form** link, and entering the details of your errata. Once your errata are verified, your submission will be accepted and the errata will be uploaded on our website, or added to any list of existing errata, under the Errata section of that title. Any existing errata can be viewed by selecting your title from http://www.packtpub.com/support.

Piracy

Piracy of copyright material on the Internet is an ongoing problem across all media. At Packt, we take the protection of our copyright and licenses very seriously. If you come across any illegal copies of our works, in any form, on the Internet, please provide us with the location address or website name immediately so that we can pursue a remedy.

Please contact us at copyright@packtpub.com with a link to the suspected pirated material.

We appreciate your help in protecting our authors, and our ability to bring you valuable content.

Questions

You can contact us at questions@packtpub.com if you are having a problem with any aspect of the book, and we will do our best to address it.

1
To Skin an App

In this chapter, you will be introduced to the PrimeFaces **JSF** (short for **JavaServer Faces**) component library, and you will create a **Maven**-based JSF web application. This application will be used throughout the book to demonstrate and test the things that we will learn in each chapter and section.

In this chapter, we will cover the following topics:

- Why we need to create an app
- An introduction to the PrimeFaces library
- Creating a Maven JSF project
- Integrating the PrimeFaces library into a Maven JSF project
- Adding the additional dependencies that GlassFish needs
- Building the project
- Running the project

Why we need to create an app

Although this book is about developing PrimeFaces themes, we will need a web application to actually test our designs. Also, a web application will be used to show how to integrate PrimeFaces into a web application and how components such as **ThemeSwitcher** are used in practice to allow a user to select their themes. Because of this, we will spend some time at the beginning creating and adding a web application to a Maven-based **NetBeans** project. When we start creating and using our own themes, the work that we will have done here will make it far easier to appreciate our creative efforts there.

The PrimeFaces library

While looking for a suitable set of **Open Source (OS)** JSF components several years ago, I discovered PrimeFaces almost by accident. What I found was a link to the PrimeFaces showcase. I was immediately impressed by the number of components that it offered and the fact that skins or themes were supported out of the box. Also, PrimeFaces uses industry-standard libraries such as **jQuery** and **jQuery UI** to make things work well and look good too. Because PrimeFaces uses the JSF standard extension framework, there are no headaches involved in integrating it into new or existing projects. In addition to providing a set of JSF components, it also provides a complete set of data model classes to support the various data-oriented components and some very useful utility classes as well. Last, but not least, PrimeFaces offers **WebSocket** support by integrating the excellent **Atmosphere** WebSocket library.

PrimeFaces also has a very active forum community, where I am often found answering questions asked by users, and hopefully getting them right too.

The version of **PrimeFaces** that I first used was 2.2, and at the time of writing this book, PrimeFaces has reached release 5.2, with 5.3 in the pipeline. The team of developers has done a wonderful job providing us with, in my opinion, the best OS JSF component library out there. It is worth paying a visit to the showcase at `http://www.primefaces.org/showcase/`, especially now that it has had a face lift and the very capable components are shown off in all their glory.

Creating a NetBeans Maven JSF project

After launching NetBeans, open the **File** menu and select **New Project** from the available project types. Locate and select **Maven**. A list of Maven archetypes (project templates) is available. Select **Web Application**, as shown in the following screenshot:

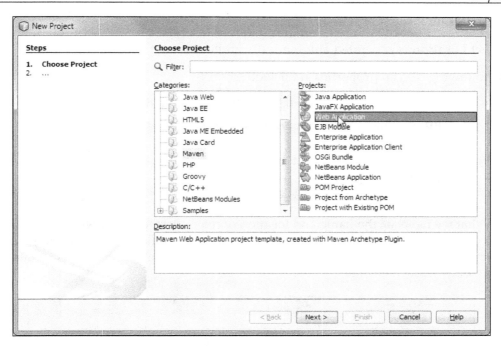

Click on **Next** and the following screenshot appears:

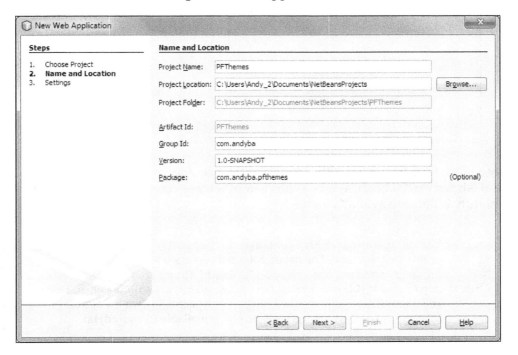

Project Name is set to PFThemes.

Project Location is generated automatically and it does not need to be changed.

The following Maven properties are listed:

- **Artifact Id**: This cannot be changed. It is the name of your project.
- **Group Id**: This can be edited as required. This sets the base package for the project.
- **Version**: This does not need to be changed.
- **Project**: This is the last property that we will use to set the root package for all the Java classes in the project.

Now that we have set the name and location of the project, click on **Next**. This leads us to the **Settings** dialog box. This is where we set the application server and Java **Enterprise Edition** (**EE**) version that we are going to use for the project, as shown in the following screenshot:

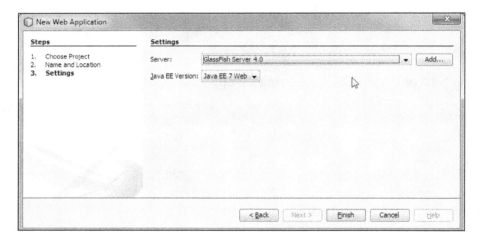

I chose **GlassFish** because it is the Java EE reference implementation. I selected **GlassFish Server 4.0** because this is the current release version of GlassFish and the nightly builds are available to me.

You can use any Java EE 7 container that supports the Java EE 7 web profile that you like. The list of potential servers is long, but **Tomcat** (http://tomcat.apache.org/), **TomEE** (http://tomee.apache.org/), and **WildFly** (http://wildfly.org/) are suitable ones. **Tomcat** and **TomEE** are freely available from the **Apache Software Foundation** (http://apache.org/)and **WildFly** is available from **RedHat**.

Once we have set the project settings, we can finish creating it. NetBeans presents us with a **Project** view containing our newly created project. If it hasn't opened a **Project** view, open the **Windows** menu and select **Projects**. You can also open a **Files** and a **Services** view. This allows us to check the files as they are built into the project, and through the **Services** view we can control things such as the GlassFish server, as well as other services such as database connections.

Now that we have successfully created the project, we have to change the project properties so that it adds the JSF framework to it.

 The JSF framework is part of the Java EE 7 standard version. It allows developers to build views/pages that are separate from the business logic and data models that make up the middle tier of data-driven applications. Because PrimeFaces builds on the facilities provided by JSF, we need to add it to our project.

Select the project and right-click on it. This opens a context menu, which allows us to perform different tasks and control various aspects of the project itself. We are interested in the one at the bottom, **Properties**. We click on it to open the **Project Properties** dialog box and select the **Frameworks** option, as shown in the following screenshot:

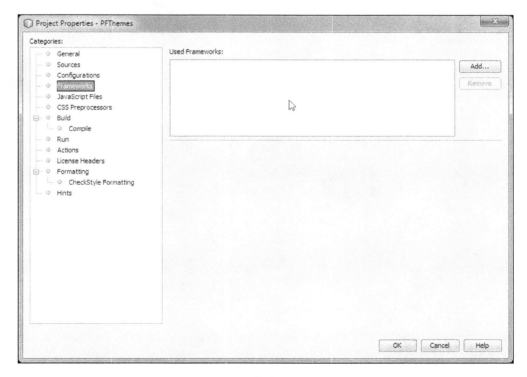

By clicking on the **Add...** button to the right, we can select a framework from a number of choices. We want JSF, so we select it and click on **OK**, as follows:

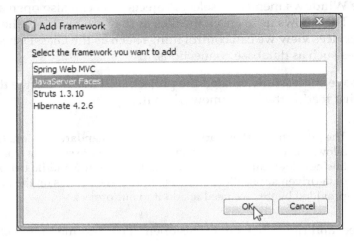

We return to the **Project Properties | Frameworks** dialog box, which looks like this:

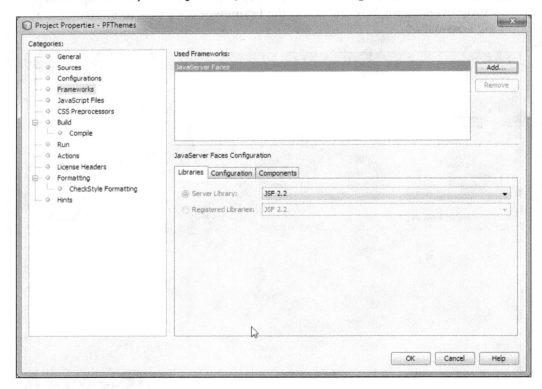

The three tabs, **Libraries**, **Configuration**, and **Components**, are used to display and/or change the configuration of the JSF framework for our project. **Libraries** cannot be altered, but it shows that we are using Java EE 7 JSF version 2.2. I also changed the configuration as follows:

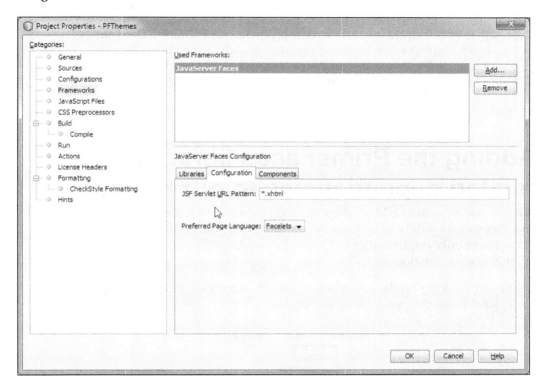

The **JSF Servlet URL Pattern** field has been changed to `*.xhtml` from the default one because it makes the linking of JSF pages easier. However, this is a purely personal preference and it is not something that you need to do.

> The **Components** tab does allow us to add the PrimeFaces library to our project. However, it adds the version bundled with NetBeans, and not the one that we will be using for our project, which is PrimeFaces 5.2 at the time of writing this book.

Once you have set up the JSF framework to your satisfaction, click on **OK**, and the changes will be applied to our project.

 While we have been doing this, NetBeans should have been building the project in the background, including the creation of the project from its Maven archetype. Maven downloads quite a large number of files when a project is created. Luckily for us, it only does this once. Maven also maintains a local repository of resources on our workstation for us so that once a file is downloaded from the **Maven Central Repository** it doesn't need to be download from there again.

Adding the PrimeFaces library and related dependencies to our project

We will use Maven to add all the required resources that we don't create ourselves, and this section will help us to understand how we add libraries to our project. PrimeFaces only requires that the PrimeFaces JAR file be added to our project. So, this is what we do:

1. By clicking on the + symbol to the left of the project in the **Project** view, we open the project tree, as follows:

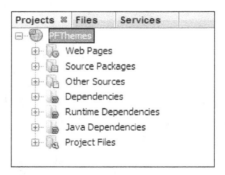

The following is a brief explanation of the folders, as listed in the previous screenshot:

- **Web Pages**: This is where we will add views or pages to our application.
- **Source Packages**: Here, Java source code is managed.

- ○ **Other Sources**: This allows us to add other types of files which may be needed for the project. We will use this facility. So, its purpose should become clear, eventually.

- ○ **Dependencies**: Here we tell Maven the JAR files that we want to add to our project.

- ○ **Runtime Dependencies** and **Java Dependencies**: These are not important for this project. Feel free to browse them at your leisure.

- ○ **Project Files**: This is where NetBeans manages both the **Maven** project's pom.xml file and the NetBeans project configuration file. While we don't need to look at these now, we will visit the pom.xml file in the later chapters. So, if you want to preview these files, please feel free to do so.

2. Meanwhile, we are going to add PrimeFaces 5.2 to our project. Right-click on the **Dependencies** folder and select **Add Dependency...** from the context menu. This opens the **Add Dependency** dialog box, as shown in the following screenshot:

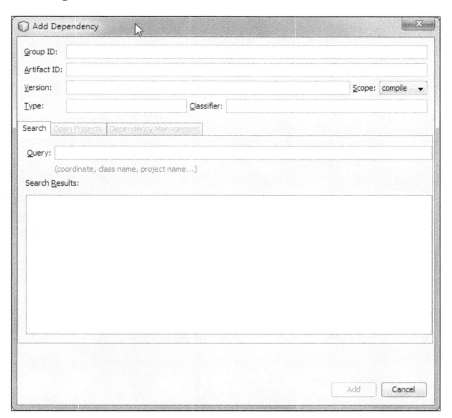

Usually, you only have the **Search** tab available in a newly created project.

 Maven allows us to add local projects as dependencies to a project, which is what the **Open Projects** tab is for. It also allows us to add dependencies that are defined in a parent **Maven** project file, and this is what the **Dependency Management** tab is for.

3. Type `org.primefaces` into the **Query** field of the **Search** tab, and then go and make a drink or something that takes a little time.

 Not only have we earned a break, but we also need time to allow Maven to download and install the Maven Central Repository index in our local Maven repository. This takes time because there are a very large number of resources available there. If you already use Maven for your projects, you obviously won't need a lot of time. The break might be welcome, though.

Once the Maven Central Repository index is available, you will see something like this:

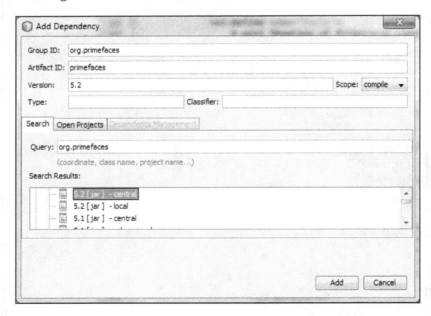

4. Select the 5.2 version and click on **Add**. Maven then adds the dependency to our project.

Building the project

When we build the project, Maven will cause the required file to be downloaded and added to our local Maven repository. It will copy the file into the WEB-INF/lib folder of the build target.

If we right-click on the project and select **Build**, Maven will do its magic. When it is finished, we can use the **Files** view to see the result. Click on the **Files** tab. Then open the project tree view. You will see an src and a target folder, as well as the project's pom.xml file and the NetBeans project configuration files.

Open the target folder. Then expand the PFThemes-1.0-SNAPSHOT folder. As we are confident that the build process will have worked correctly, we can now see the structure of the web application:

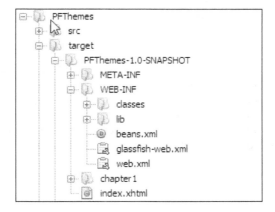

The Java EE 7 standard mandates a formal folder structure for web applications. The META-INF and WEB-INF folders are where application-specific resources are stored. Under WEB-INF, you will see a classes folder, a lib folder, and several configuration files. Don't worry if you don't see any or all of the configuration files. Only web.xml is generated by default; the others will be created later in this chapter. The classes folder is to where Java classes are compiled. The lib folder is where JAR files, such as the PrimeFaces JAR file, are added.

Although PrimeFaces does not require any additional dependencies, GlassFish does check each JAR file for optional dependencies and treats them as mandatory ones. Because of this rather petty strictness, we also need to add the `commons-fileupload` and `commons-io` dependencies. These are only required for the PrimeFaces `fileupload` component, which won't be used here. At the time of writing this book, GlassFish does not allow applications to be run with unsatisfied dependencies. So, we need to add the missing dependencies.

Add a dependency as you did before, but this time type in `commons-fileupload` in the query field and select version **1.3.1**. Don't forget to click on **Add** before adding the `commons-io` dependency. For this, you select the **2.1** version.

Running the project

Now build the project again. After the build is finished, right-click on the project and select **Run**.

This causes the GlassFish server to run and our application to be deployed. Once the project is deployed, NetBeans then opens its default browser and points it to the application's start page.

I use Google Chrome as my NetBeans default browser because NetBeans provides a Chrome plugin that allows us to debug scripts in our pages as well as other useful services. I am not going to force you to use a particular browser, but I do recommend that you use Google Chrome for the aforementioned reasons. The only browser-related thing that you should avoid is using Internet Explorer below version 8. The latest JSF technologies are not guaranteed to work with the older Internet Explorer versions, and the visual experience, even with Internet Explorer 8, is underwhelming compared to modern browsers.

We should see something like this in Chrome:

Now that we have got the project running, we can add the other configuration files that we saw in an earlier screenshot.

Summary

Well done. You made it to the end of the first chapter with a working project and learned the repeatable steps that are required to create any PrimeFaces JSF web project using Maven.

In this chapter, we have successfully created a NetBeans Maven web project using the new project wizard, added the JSF framework to the project by adjusting the **Project Properties**, added the PrimeFaces component library as a dependency using Maven, added additional libraries as dependencies using Maven, and finally ran the project in GlassFish and viewed the start page of the application in a browser.

These steps are always the first steps that we need to take when creating a new PrimeFaces and JSF-based web application. Because of this, I felt that it's important that the first chapter of this book is devoted to this rather than the more fun things that we will be getting into later in the book.

2
Introducing PrimeFaces Themes

In order to be able to experience using JSF and the PrimeFaces library, we are going to continue our work from the last chapter and add to the PFThemes project. By the end of this chapter, you will have a deeper understanding of how even a simple JSF application can be greatly enriched by using PrimeFaces components in it. In particular, I will demonstrate how PrimeFaces provides a powerful themes framework.

In this chapter, we will cover the following topics:

- The difference between standard JSF and PrimeFaces components
- Adding additional themes to the project
- Changing the theme used by the project
- Displaying the name of the theme used by the project
- Adding some classes to allow us to use the ThemeSwitcher component
- Changing web.xml so that it supports dynamic themes
- Creating a Facelets Template and adding a menu for navigation and a ThemeSwitcher to it
- Creating a page that uses this template and adding some components to it
- Adding a link to this page in the template
- Displaying the name of the theme that is currently being used in the template
- Adding some buttons to the page to switch themes without using the ThemeSwitcher

The difference between standard JSF and PrimeFaces components

Standard JSF components such as h:inputText result in simple HTML being emitted into the page. To demonstrate what I mean, you need to perform the following steps:

1. Create a JSF page in your project in a new folder called chapter2 and name the page difference.xhtml.

2. To create the folder, right-click on the **Web Pages** folder in the **Project** navigator and move the mouse over the **New** item. Select the **Folder** option, name the folder chapter2, and click on **Finish**.

3. Then, right-click on the chapter2 folder, move the mouse over the **New** item, and select **JSF Page**. Name the page difference and click on **Finish**.

 NetBeans will add the appropriate file ending for you. So, if you type in difference.xhtml, the file will actually be named difference.xhtml.xhtml. So you don't need to add the extension explicitly.

We then add the following inside the h:body tag:

```
<h:form id="mainform">
  <h:panelGrid id="maintable" columns="2">
  <h:outputLabel id="simpleLabel1" value="A standard inputText
    component:" for="standardInput"/>
  <h:inputText id="standardInput"/>
  <p:outputLabel id="pfLabel2" value="A PrimeFaces inputText
    component:" for="pfInput"/>
  <p:inputText id="pfInput"/>
  </h:panelGrid>
</h:form>
```

NetBeans will give you a hint indicating that you need to add the PrimeFaces namespace declaration to the page by displaying a small *red lamp* icon to the left of the affected line. By clicking on the *lamp* icon, NetBeans prompts you to add the appropriate namespace.

Now, run the project and type http://localhost:8080/PFThemes/chapter2/difference.xhtml in the browser that NetBeans opens.

This is what you will see:

As you can see, the standard JSF components cause standard html to be added to the page. The PrimeFaces components do the same, but they look different. This is because PrimeFaces uses a default theme, which uses CSS to set the look and feel of the components in the browser.

If you use Google Chrome to view the page, you can also inspect the elements that you see on the page by right-clicking on one of them, such as the standard inputText component, and clicking on the **Inspect element** menu option.

This is how the HTML for the h:inputText field looks:

```
<input id="mainform:standardInput" type="text"
    name="mainform:standardInput">
```

Apart from the ID that JSF creates for us based on the parent component IDs, there is nothing unusual about it.

Now, do the same for the lower p:outputLabel, element. You should see the following HTML:

```
<label id="mainform:pfLabel2" class="ui-outputlabel ui-widget"
    for="mainform:pfInput">A PrimeFaces inputText component:</label>
```

Look at the class attribute; there are some CSS classes added. It is these CSS rules that PrimeFaces uses not only for structural settings, dimensions, and so on, but also to set the way they appear visually. It is here that we begin to see how a PrimeFaces theme works.

 The names of the CSS rules are the same regardless of which theme is being used. Having predictable CSS rule names makes it very easy to apply themes to a PrimeFaces application.

Now, let's inspect the p:inputText field:

```
<input id="mainform:pfInput" name="mainform:pfInput" type="text"
  class="ui-inputfield ui-inputtext ui-widget ui-state-default ui-
  corner-all" role="textbox" aria-disabled="false" aria-
  readonly="false">
```

Here, we see that not only does PrimeFaces set the CSS rules in the class attribute, and quite a few of them too; but it also adds things like the role and aria attributes as well. The use of the role and aria attributes is important for accessibility. **Screen readers**, used by people with impaired vision, understand these attributes and can read them out so that users know that there is a component that they can interact with. This is another very strong point in PrimeFaces' favor.

Adding additional PrimeFaces themes

In this section, we are going to turn to the power of Maven to add additional themes. We can do this because the PrimeFaces team has made them available as dependencies. The only difference here is that they haven't made them available on Maven Central Repository. Instead, they are available on PrimeFaces Maven repository.

 Did you know that anyone can set up a Maven repository for themselves and provide libraries to the public? Doing this means not having to wait to get your work added to Maven Central Repository.

In order to get Maven to point to the PrimeFaces repository, we need to add an entry in the project's pom.xml file.

Open the pom.xml file, which will be found in the project's **Project Files** folder. Under the name tag (highlighted in the following code), add everything in the repositories tag and save the file:

```
<name>PFThemes</name>
<repositories>
  <repository>
    <id>prime-repo</id>
    <name>PrimeFaces Maven Repository</name>
    <url>http://repository.primefaces.org</url>
    <layout>default</layout>
  </repository>
</repositories>
```

Now, after doing this, we can add additional themes as dependencies to our project. In the `pom.xml` file, scroll down until you find the `dependencies` tag. We will now add a dependency for the **bootstrap theme**.

By adding the following snippet of XML to the `pom` project, we add all the openly available PrimeFaces themes to the project:

```
<dependency>
    <groupId>org.primefaces.themes</groupId>
    <artifactId>all-themes</artifactId>
    <version>1.0.10</version>
</dependency>
```

By building the project, we cause Maven to download the `theme.jar` file and add it to the project's runtime.

What happens when we run the project? Try it and see what happens. Navigate to the `difference.xhtml` page that we created earlier. Is anything different now that we have added the bootstrap theme?

The theme being used is still the default theme — **aristo**. So, we obviously need to tell the project to use the new one. Fortunately, PrimeFaces makes this very easy for us.

We need to open the `web.xml` file and add the following XML code:

```
<context-param>
    <param-name>primefaces.THEME</param-name>
    <param-value>bootstrap</param-value>
</context-param>
```

Now, save the changes and rerun, build, and run the project.

 NetBeans can deploy your project when you save files in it. In the project properties sheet, select the **Run** option and check off the **Deploy** on save checkbox.

Refresh the `difference.xhtml` page. See the changes? We can display the value of the theme setting in our page. You need to add the following highlighted code to `difference.xhtml` before the `</h:panelGrid>` tag page:

```
<h:outputText id="currentThemeLabel" value="Current theme"/>
<h:outputText id="currentThemeValue" value=
    "#{initParam['primefaces.THEME']}"/>
</h:panelGrid>
```

Refresh the `difference.xhtml` page in your browser and you should see the current theme bootstrap.

We can not only set the theme for our project, but also change it while the project is running. Furthermore, we can allow users to choose which theme they wish to use without affecting the choices that other users make.

The PrimeFaces ThemeSwitcher component

PrimeFaces provides a component called **ThemeSwitcher**, which allows us to change themes dynamically without having to refresh the page that we are on. In order to get this to work, we need to create some classes known as **JavaBeans**, which provide things that the ThemeSwitcher needs in order to work its magic.

We are going to add some new packages to our project and then create our Beans. Perform the following steps to add new packages to our project:

1. Right-click on the project in the **Project** view and select **New...**.
2. You may have to scroll down a bit or even select the **Other...** option, but we are looking for the Java option. This displays a list of things that we can create, and we want a package.
3. We add a package with the name `com.andyba.pfthemes.session` keeping the other values as they are.
4. Then, add another package named **com.andyba.pfthemes.themes**.

Now, in order to create our first Bean, perform the following steps:

1. Select **New...** by right-clicking on the themes package menu (open the **Sources** tree from the project) and look for JSF Managed Bean. The following dialog box opens:

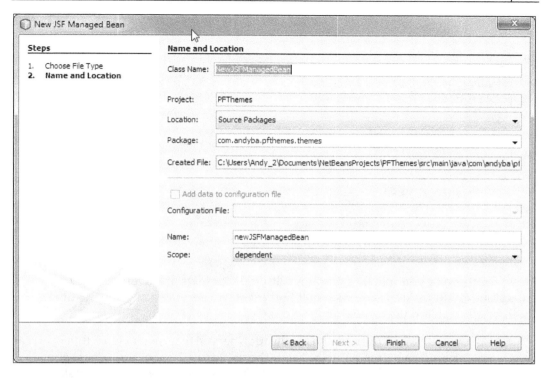

2. Change the **Class Name** field to `ThemesService`. When you do this, the **Name** field changes automatically. You can leave this field as it is.

3. Change the **Scope** field to **Application** and then click on **Finish**.

The source code file for the `ThemesService` Bean is then opened by NetBeans, and it should look like this:

```
package com.andyba.pfthemes.themes;

import java.util.logging.Logger;
import javax.inject.Named;
import javax.enterprise.context.ApplicationScoped;
```

```
/**
 *
 * @author Andy_2
 */
@ManagedBean@ApplicationScoped
public class ThemesService {

  private static final Logger logger =
    Logger.getLogger(ThemesService.class.getName());

  /**
   * Creates a new instance of ThemesService
   */
  public ThemesService() {

}
```

Now, for those of you who are familiar with JSF **Contexts and Dependency Injection (CDI)**, the annotations won't be a mystery. For those of you who are not, I will briefly explain the following:

- @ManagedBean: This tells the application server that instances of this Bean can be referred to by the name as set in the value attribute of the annotation. This means that we can use the name in JSF pages to magically access instances of our Bean.

- @ApplicationScoped: This annotation tells the application server that only one instance of the ThemesService Bean needs to be created and that it shall remain available for the entire time that the application is running. We only need one because we will use the Bean to provide a list of theme choices to the next Bean that we create, the CurrentTheme Bean.

Creating the CurrentTheme Bean

Right-click on the session package, this time click on **New...**, and select the **JSF Managed Bean** option again.

 Did you notice that NetBeans remembers the menu options you chose recently and moves them to the top of the options list? NetBeans is fantastic.

Name the class as `CurrentTheme` and change **Scope** to **Session**. The source code is once again opened automatically for us and it looks like this:

```
package com.andyba.pfthemes.session;

*/
import java.io.Serializable;
import javax.inject.Named;
import javax.enterprise.context.SessionScoped;

/**
 *
 * @author Andy_2
 */
@ManagedBean
@SessionScoped
public class CurrentTheme implements
Serializable {

    /**
     * Creates a new instance of CurrentTheme
     */
    public CurrentTheme() {
    }
}
```

There is a new annotation, `@SessionScoped`, which needs to be explained now:

`@SessionScoped`: A session-scoped Bean is one that is created each time a user visits the application for the first time and lives for as long as the user session is valid. A **session** remains valid as long as the user actively uses the application. This way, we can use this Bean to keep track of information such as user preferences. Now, in a real-life application, we will store things such as user preferences in a database and have the user log in to our application so that we can read the preferences from the database.

The user preference that we are going to keep track of is the theme that the user chooses. We are now going to create a property for our Bean called `theme`. In the Bean source code window, move the cursor to the line after the curly brace, as follows:

```
    public CurrentTheme() {
    }
// Cursor here
```

Press the *Tab* key once, right-click on the location where the cursor is, and select the **Insert code...** option. From the context menu that opens, select **Add property...**. On doing this, the following dialog box opens:

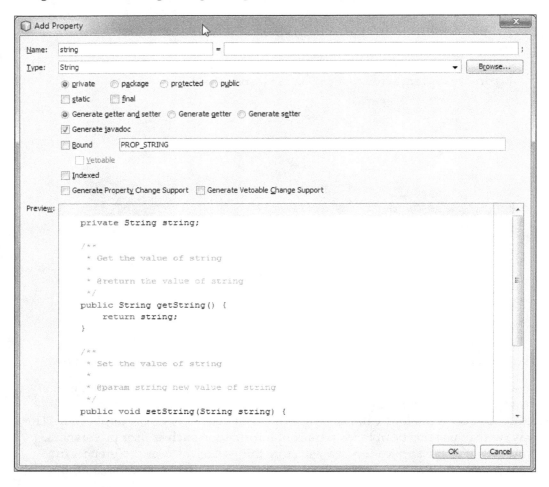

Change the name from string to theme. Then, add "aristo" in the text field to the right of the = sign. We can leave the rest of the dialog box settings as they are and click on **OK**.

The following code is added to our Bean:

```
private String theme = "aristo";

/**
* @return the theme
*/
public String getTheme() {
  return theme;
}

/**
* @param theme the theme to set
*/
public void setTheme(String theme) {
  this.theme = theme;
}
```

Remember that `aristo` is the name of the default theme and we want to use this as the default user theme preference. Now, we need to tell the project how to use the Bean `theme` property value to set the name of the theme being currently employed by the user.

The `context` parameter that we used to set the bootstrap theme in the `web.xml` project needs to be changed to access the `CurrentTheme` Bean. Open the `web.xml` file, locate the `context` parameter entry that we added earlier, and change the parameter value according to the highlighted value in the following code:

```
<context-param>
  <param-name>primefaces.THEME</param-name>
  <param-value>#{currentTheme.theme}</param-value>
</context-param>
```

If you go back to the `difference.xhtml` page, you will see that the name of the theme has been changed to `#{currentTheme.theme}`, which isn't what we actually want. Change the last `outputText` tag value attribute to the following:

```
value="#{currentTheme.theme}"
```

Refresh the page. Now, you will see that `aristo` is the name of the current theme. Note that the theme has changed back to aristo as well.

Extending the ThemeService Bean

In order to get the ThemeSwitcher to work, we need to provide a list of theme names that ThemeSwitcher uses to offer the user a choice of themes. We will do this in the `ThemeService` Bean as an extension to the services it provides.

 As the Bean is application scoped, there is only one instance of it during the lifetime of the application. Thus, we are saving valuable resources by doing so.

We will add a new property to the Bean in a manner that is similar to how we added the `theme` property to the `CurrentTheme` Bean. The completely filled out **Add Property** dialog box is shown in the following screenshot:

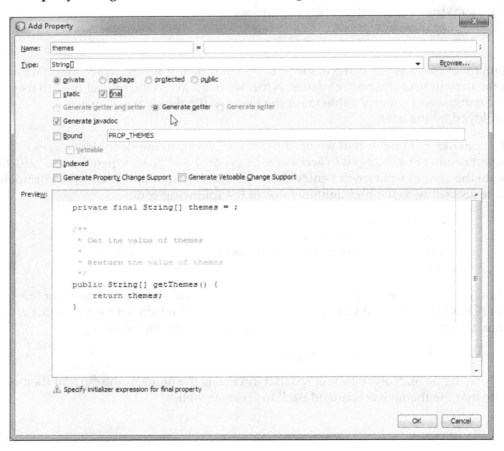

The `themes` property is an array because it will never be modified at runtime. Hence, it is a read-only property and hence the `final` keyword.

Place the cursor after `private final String[] themes =` but before `;`. Then, add the following code to initialize the array. The added code is highlighted for you:

```
private final String[] themes = {"afterdark",
    "afternoon",
    "afterwork",
    "aristo",
    "black-tie",
    "blitzer",
    "bluesky",
    "bootstrap",
    "casablanca",
    "cupertino",
    "cruze",
    "dark-hive",
    "delta",
    "dot-luv",
    "eggplant",
    "excite-bike",
    "flick",
    "glass-x",
    "home",
    "hot-sneaks",
    "humanity",
    "le-frog",
    "midnight",
    "mint-choc",
    "overcast",
    "pepper-grinder",
    "redmond",
    "rocket",
    "sam",
    "smoothness",
    "south-street",
    "start",
    "sunny",
    "swanky-purse",
    "trontastic",
    "ui-darkness",
    "ui-lightness",
    "vader"};
```

Don't forget to save the changes.

For more information about PrimeFaces themes, visit http://primefaces.org/ themes We are now going to create a **Facelets Template** and add elements to it, which are what we want to see in each page that we create using it. As it is common in web applications, we want the navigation elements to appear in each page along with the possible status information and, for this project, a ThemeSwitcher.

Creating a Facelets Template

Because templates are not pages in themselves, we don't want them to be accessible as a page. In order to do this, we need to create it in the WEB-INF folder.

 The **JEE7 standard** stipulates that the WEB-INF folder and all of its contents must be inaccessible on a browser for users.

We need to keep things organized and place things such as template files separate from configuration files such as web.xml. So, we will create a folder named resources in the WEB-INF folder and then create another folder in the resources folder named templates. Perform the following steps to create a Facelets Template:

1. In the **Projects** navigator, open the WEB-INF folder and then select it. You should see something similar to the following screenshot:

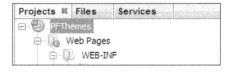

2. Right-click on the WEB-INF folder, move the mouse over the **New** item, and select **Folder...**, as shown in the following screenshot:

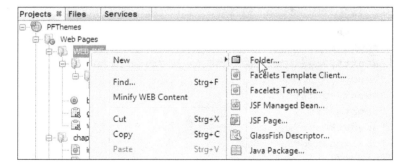

3. Name the new folder `resources`. Next, create a new folder and name it `templates`. The `WEB-INF` folder should look similar to what's shown in the following screenshot:

4. We are now going to create a Facelets Template and modify it to remove the elements that we don't need. Right-click on the `templates` folder and move the mouse over the **Facelets Template...** item. If the **Facelets Template...** option is not visible, you will have to navigate to **Other... | JavaServer Faces | Facelets Template...**.The dialog box that opens when you do this is shown in the following screenshot:

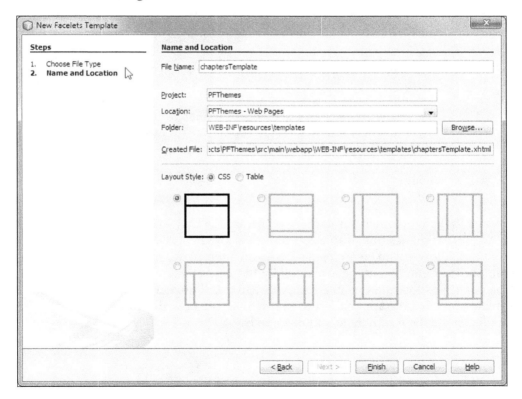

5. Call the `chaptersTemplate` template and leave the other options as they are with their default settings. When you open the `template` file or when NetBeans opens it for you, you will see the following code:

```
<?xml version='1.0' encoding='UTF-8' ?>
<!DOCTYPE html PUBLIC "-//W3C//DTD XHTML 1.0
  Transitional//EN" "http://www.w3.org/TR/xhtml1/DTD/
  xhtml1-transitional.dtd">
<html
  xmlns="http://www.w3.org/1999/xhtml"
  xmlns:ui="http://xmlns.jcp.org/jsf/facelets"
  xmlns:h="http://xmlns.jcp.org/jsf/html">
  <h:head>
    <meta http-equiv="Content-Type" content="text/html;
        charset=UTF-8" />
    <h:outputStylesheet name="./css/default.css"/>
    <h:outputStylesheet name="./css/cssLayout.css"/>
    <title>Facelets Template</title>
  </h:head>
  <h:body>

    <div id="top" class="top">
      <ui:insert name="top">Top</ui:insert>
    </div>

    <div id="content" class="center_content">
      <ui:insert name="content">Content</ui:insert>
    </div>

  </h:body>
</html>
```

The page looks very much similar to the normal XHTML and in fact, it is a normal XHTML. What makes this usable as a template are the `<ui:insert>` tags. The JSF framework allows us to create pages based on a template, and `define` tags are used to replace the default content contained by the `insert` tags, with the content specific to the page. To illustrate this in a better way, we will now create a page that uses this template and runs the application so that we can see how this looks. After doing this, we will change the template to suit our needs.

To create the **Facelets Template Client,** right-click on the **Web Files** folder in the **Project** navigation, move the mouse over the **New** item, and select **Facelets Template Client**. The resulting dialog box is shown in the following screenshot. If the Facelets Template Client option is not available, then you will have to choose **Other...**, **JavaServer Faces,** and then select **Facelets Template Client**:

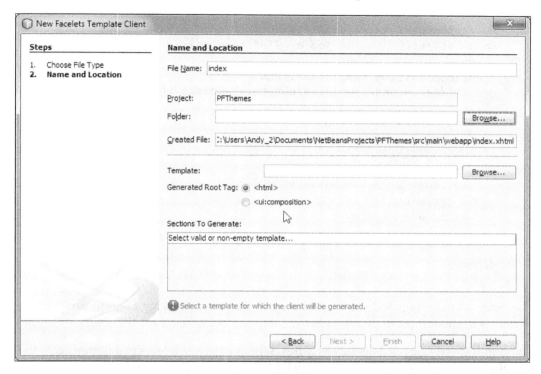

Call the index page. Then, select the template that you want to use by browsing for it. Click on the **Browse** button to the right of **Template:** and select the chaptersTemplate template that we created earlier.

If you already have an XHTML page called index, you will need to rename it first.

After clicking on **Finish**, NetBeans will open the newly create page to reveal the following code:

```
<?xml version='1.0' encoding='UTF-8' ?>
<!DOCTYPE html PUBLIC "-//W3C//DTD XHTML 1.0 Transitional//EN"
  "http://www.w3.org/TR/xhtml1/DTD/xhtml1-transitional.dtd">
<html
  xmlns="http://www.w3.org/1999/xhtml"
  xmlns:ui="http://xmlns.jcp.org/jsf/facelets">
  <body>
    <ui:composition template="./WEB-
      INF/resources/templates/chaptersTemplate.xhtml">

      <ui:define name="top">
        top
      </ui:define>

      <ui:define name="content">
        content
      </ui:define>

    </ui:composition>
  </body>
</html>
```

The composition tags tell the JSF framework that the following content replaces elements in the template. It also sets the template being used for this page.

The highlighted define tags have names, which match the insert tag names in the template. This is how the JSF framework builds pages using templates.

If you run the project, you will see the following in the browser:

As you can see, NetBeans has added some kind of theme to the page via the template. We can also see that the page title comes from the template and not the page itself. The changes that we are now going to make to the template will remove references to the CSS files that we are not going to use and add an `insert` component for a title.

We will also remove the `div` tags in the template that provide structure to the page, which is also not needed by us.

Open the `chaptersTemplate` file and remove the `<h:outputStylesheet name="./ css/cssLayout.css"/>` tag. We also want to delete the `cssLayout.css` file, as we do not need it anymore.

 JSF enables us to reference resources such as CSS and images without actually knowing where they are located. It does this by searching for the resources in special folders. These special folders are named `resources` and can be located either directly in the application's root folder or in the `WEB-INF` folder. It is no accident that we named the `resources` folder in `WEB-INF` the way we did.

NetBeans created `default.css` and `cssLayout.css` for us. Here, we see NetBeans applying best practices in that it separates structural and theme elements into `cssLayout.css`, which has rules that specify things such as the dimensions of containers, and `default.css`, which has rules that specify things such as fonts and foreground and background colors. PrimeFaces also applies this best practice, which makes creating custom themes much easier, as we will soon see.

Now, open the `default.css` file, select the entire contents, and delete it all, saving the file afterwards. In the `title` tag, add an `insert` tag with the name title. The default content should be `Please add a proper title for this page!`.

The changes that you have made so far should look like this:

```
<?xml version='1.0' encoding='UTF-8' ?>
<!DOCTYPE html PUBLIC "-//W3C//DTD XHTML 1.0 Transitional//EN"
  "http://www.w3.org/TR/xhtml1/DTD/xhtml1-transitional.dtd">
<html
  xmlns="http://www.w3.org/1999/xhtml"
  xmlns:ui="http://xmlns.jcp.org/jsf/facelets"
  xmlns:h="http://xmlns.jcp.org/jsf/html">
  <h:head>
    <meta http-equiv="Content-Type" content="text/html;
      charset=UTF-8" />
```

```
<h:outputStylesheet name="./css/default.css"/>
<title>

    <ui:insert name="title">Please add a proper title for this
        page!</ui:insert>

</title>
</h:head>
<h:body>

    <div id="top" class="top">
      <ui:insert name="top">Top</ui:insert>
    </div>

    <div id="content" class="center_content">
      <ui:insert name="content">Content</ui:insert>
    </div>

</h:body>
</html>
```

If you now save the template and refresh the page in the browser, you will see something similar to the following screenshot:

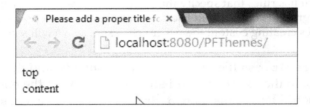

By removing the reference to the `cssLayout.css` file and emptying the `default.css` file, you changed how the page looks. The background colors are gone, and the font used is the browser default, which is usually **Times New Roman**.

Although you haven't added a title using a `define` tag for the `index.xhtml` file, the default content from the template is used. Now, open the `index.xhtml` file and add a `define` tag, whose content should be `Welcome to Developing PrimeFaces Themes`.

The code now looks like this:

```
<?xml version='1.0' encoding='UTF-8' ?>
<!DOCTYPE html PUBLIC "-//W3C//DTD XHTML 1.0 Transitional//EN"
  "http://www.w3.org/TR/xhtml1/DTD/xhtml1-transitional.dtd">
<html
  xmlns="http://www.w3.org/1999/xhtml"
  xmlns:ui="http://xmlns.jcp.org/jsf/facelets">
  <body>

    <ui:composition template="./WEB-
      INF/resources/templates/chaptersTemplate.xhtml">

      <ui:define name="title">Welcome to Developing PrimeFaces
        Themes</ui:define>

      <ui:define name="top">
        top
      </ui:define>

      <ui:define name="content">
        content
      </ui:define>

    </ui:composition>

  </body>
</html>
```

The page title code that we added is highlighted. Note that it is not important where the `define` tags are placed. The only important thing that you need to remember is that they must be contained by the `composition` tag. When you save the page and refresh it in your browser, you will see something similar to the following:

Now, go back to the Facelets Template and replace its contents with the following code:

```
<?xml version='1.0' encoding='UTF-8' ?>
<!DOCTYPE html PUBLIC "-//W3C//DTD XHTML 1.0 Transitional//EN"
  "http://www.w3.org/TR/xhtml1/DTD/xhtml1-transitional.dtd">
<html
  xmlns="http://www.w3.org/1999/xhtml"
  xmlns:ui="http://xmlns.jcp.org/jsf/facelets"
  xmlns:h="http://xmlns.jcp.org/jsf/html"
  xmlns:p="http://primefaces.org/ui"
  xmlns:f="http://xmlns.jcp.org/jsf/core">
<f:view contentType="text/html" encoding="UTF-8">
  <h:head>
    <meta http-equiv="Content-Type" content="text/html;
      charset=UTF-8" />
    <f:facet name="last">
      <h:outputStylesheet library="css" name="default.css"/>
    </f:facet>
    <title>
      <ui:insert name="title">Please add a proper title for this
        page!</ui:insert>
    </title>
  </h:head>

  <h:body>
    <h:form id="navForm">
      <p:menubar id="navBar">
        <p:menuitem id="home" value="Home" url="/index.xhtml"/>
          <p:submenu id="chapter2" label="Chapter 2">
            <p:menuitem id="c2difference" value="Differences"
              url="/chapter2/difference.xhtml"/>
          </p:submenu>
        <f:facet name="options">
          <h:outputText value="Current theme: " style="vertical-
            align: top;"/>
          <h:outputText value="#{currentTheme.theme} "
            style="vertical-align: top;"/>
          <p:themeSwitcher id="themeSwitcher" effect="fade"
            value="#{currentTheme.theme}">
            <f:selectItem itemLabel="Choose Theme" itemValue=""
              itemDisabled="true"/>
```

```
            <f:selectItems value="#{themesService.themes}"
              var="theme" itemLabel="#{theme}"
              itemValue="#{theme}" itemLabelEscaped="true"/>
            <p:ajax update="@form"/>
          </p:themeSwitcher>
        </f:facet>
      </p:menubar>
    </h:form>
    <p:panel id="content" style="text-align: center">
      <ui:insert name="content">Content</ui:insert>
    </p:panel>
  </h:body>

  </f:view>
</html>
```

The `view` tag is used to instruct the browser about the type of content for the page and its character encoding.

> The `view` tag isn't strictly needed. However, some browsers will not display certain content correctly if we don't use it. Hence, we use it here. It should be used in every JSF page for every JSF project. Remember that it also needs to enclose the `head` and `body` tags of the page.

The `facet` tag with the `name="last"` attribute tells PrimeFaces where to generate the HTML code for the CSS file reference in the head section of the page after any others that JSF and/or PrimeFaces generates.

The `<h:outputStylesheet library="css" name="default.css"/>` tag loads the `default.css` file from the CSS library. The *Oracle JSF Tutorial* explains what this means in detail. Basically, folders in a `resources` folder are treated as libraries of resources. Hence, we used `library="css"` and `name="default.css"`.

> The JSF specification does not specify which order resource references such as this are to be in the page. This means that PrimeFaces-generated resource references can appear before or after the ones that we use in our pages. This makes using the *cascading* part of CSS impossible. To solve this problem, PrimeFaces takes over the responsibility of generating the resource reference HTML from JSF and allows us to specify the order in which our references should be generated in relation to those that PrimeFaces and other component libraries generate. The order is specified using facets with the `name="last"` or `name="first"` attributes.

We added navigation elements to the template. Active elements like this need to be contained by a `form` tag. The ThemeSwitcher component also needs to be contained within a form.

Because this is a book about PrimeFaces themes, it is only right that we use the PrimeFaces navigation component named `menubar`. Contained within the `menubar` is a `menuitem`, which links to the start page of our project and a submenu for **Chapter 2**. At this point, the **Chapter 2** submenu only contains one link to the `differences.xhtml` page. By default, the menu bar aligns its child elements to the left.

The `<f:facet name="options">` tag allows us to add components to the right of the `menubar`. Inside this facet, we have two `outputText` tags, which set the `Current theme` label and the name of the theme that is currently selected by the user.

Also contained in this facet is the ThemeSwitcher component as well as the `selectItem` and `selectItems` tags that configure it.

If you look at the `outputText` tag, which displays the name of the currently selected theme, its value attribute contains code similar to the code used in `web.xml` to set the current theme for the application.

Code in `web.xml`:

```
<context-param>
  <param-name>primefaces.THEME</param-name>
  <param-value>#{currentTheme.theme}</param-value>
</context-param>
```

The `outputText` tag is as follows:

```
<h:outputText value="#{currentTheme.theme} " style="vertical-
  align: top;"/>
```

This is no coincidence. **EL** (short for **Expression Language**) expressions are used to wire up the frontend of an application (the pages) with the Beans that we use in the application's middle layer.

One of the biggest problems with the JSP framework was that it allowed developers to mix server-side business logic with the display elements in the code. This led to a project that was very hard to maintain and it also meant that web developers and the developers who write the business logic occupied the same real estate as it were. JSF now makes this impossible by not allowing any server-side code to be embedded in the page, forcing the Beans developers and the web developers apart. This not only makes for more easily maintainable projects, but also means that Beans developers who don't require knowledge of the frontend can maintain code that is separate from the web developers who don't need any knowledge of Java at all. The glue that allows you to bind properties and method calls for AJAX requests is EL. A complete explanation of EL expressions and JSF is beyond the scope of this book. Oracle published a JSF 2.2 tutorial, which can be found at `https://docs.oracle.com/javaee/7/tutorial/`.

After saving the template, you can now go back to the `index.xhtml` file and simply remove the define `name="top"` tag and its contents. Save your changes and then refresh the page in the browser. With luck, you will see something similar to the following screenshot:

If the page doesn't looks like this or it doesn't appear at all, you may need to clean and build the project before running it again.

The ThemeSwitcher component to the right of the page can now be used to change the theme being used. Here is a screenshot, with the **le-frog** theme selected:

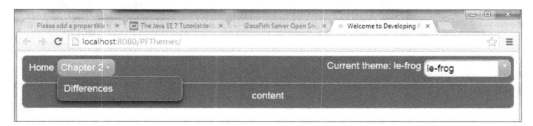

You may have noted that changing the theme does not require the entire page to be reloaded. The magic happens in the browser with a small AJAX request, which causes the value for the `theme` property in the `CurrentTheme` Bean to be set and another one, which updates the navigation section of the page. Because we only have the word **content** in the content section of the page, the savings in network traffic are not very big, but imagine a page with a lot of components and displayed information in the content section of the page.

As you can see, you managed to build in some rather complicated features into the pages with minimum effort. JSF is a very powerful technology in itself, and one of the most powerful features is its extensibility. The PrimeFaces developers used this extensibility to provide us with a component library that makes adding these otherwise complicated features easy.

We are now going to create a page based on `chaptersTemplate` in the `chapter2` folder.

Then, we are going to add several PrimeFaces components to this page so that we can demonstrate how things look across several themes. Last but not least, we are going to add three buttons and make those buttons change the current theme without using the ThemeSwitcher. We are also going to add a link to that page in `chaptersTemplate`, clean and build the project, and run it anew.

Creating a Mini Showcase page

In the following section, we will create pages with PrimeFaces components so that we can see how themes affect their look and feel. It is a **mini showcase** because we will not add every available PrimeFaces component.

Perform the following steps to create a Mini Showcase page:

1. Right-click on the `chapter2` folder and move the mouse over **New**. Select the **Facelets Template Client** option and name it `morecomponents`.

 For the book, we are developing a project that will be used to show off our own theme. This project is available in a GIT repository (see the *Preface* for the link). The file names that I used are those that I used in that project. You are of course free to choose your own filenames.

2. Choose `chaptersTemplate` as the page template and click on **Finish**.

3. Add an appropriate page title in the `define name="title"` tag. I used the following:

```
<ui:define name="title">
  A mini ShowCase of PrimeFaces components
</ui:define>
```

4. Then, add the following code in the content `define` tag. I included the `define` tag for completeness; the relevant code is highlighted:

```
<ui:define name="content">

  <h:form id="mainForm">
    <h:panelGrid columns="2">
      <p:outputLabel value="PrimeFaces Input:"/><p:inputText/>
      <p:outputLabel value="PrimeFaces Spinner"/><p:spinner/>
      <p:outputLabel value="PrimeFaces Panel"/>
      <p:panel header="An simple panel" toggleable="true"
        toggleTitle="Click to close/open">
        <p:commandButton value="Show dialog" onclick=
          "PF('simpleDialog').show();"process="@this"/>
      </p:panel>
    </h:panelGrid>
    <p:dataList value="#{themesService.themes}" var="theme">
      #{theme}
    </p:dataList>
    <p:dialog id="dialog1" widgetVar="simpleDialog"
      modal="true">
      <p:commandButton id="closeDialog" value="Close the
        dialog" onclick="PF('simpleDialog').hide();"
        process="@this"/>
    </p:dialog>
  </h:form>

</ui:define>
```

There is no need to go into the different components here. The important thing is that we have a set of components with different features that will look different according to the theme currently being used.

5. Save the file and open `chaptersTemplate`. Then, add a link to the page that we just created by adding the following highlighted code to the **Chapter 2** submenu:

```
<p:submenu id="chapter2" label="Chapter 2">
  <p:menuitem id="c2difference" value="Differences"
    url="/chapter2/difference.xhtml"/>
  <p:menuitem id="c2morecomponents" value="Mini Showcase"
    url="/chapter2/morecomponents.xhtml"/>
</p:submenu>
```

6. Now, save the changes that we made. To make sure that the project runs correctly, we need to clean and build the project before running it again.

7. When the project is up and running again, use the **Chapter 2** submenu to navigate to the **Mini Showcase** page. You will see something similar to the following screenshot:

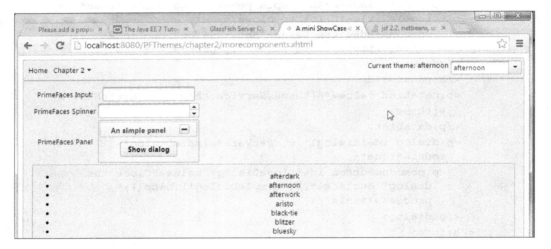

In the preceding screenshot, the **afternoon** theme was chosen. This is a good opportunity if you wish to try out the different available themes to see how things look.

The **Show dialog** button actually opens a modal dialog box, which contains a button to close the dialog box again. Try it to see how the dialog box looks. Note that we cannot change the current theme with the dialog box left open. This is because a modal dialog box masks the rest of the page and only allows interaction with the dialog box itself. We use a modal dialog box here because of the pane used to mask the rest of the page. It normally has a translucent background, but this can change depending on the theme.

Adding buttons that change the theme without using ThemeSwitcher

We are now going to add code to the `morecomponents.xhtml` page, which allows us to switch themes without using the ThemeSwitcher component. We are going to add them at the end because the code needs to be explained so that you have a clear understanding of how this is done. I chose `commandButton` for the task, but we just as easily could have used other components that support the `action` attribute and have the ability to cause the page to be requested in full or allow us to update the entire page using an AJAX request.

Here is the code that we need to add immediately after the `form` tag with `id="mainform"`:

```
<p:panelGrid columns="3">
  <p:column>
    <p:commandButton ajax="false" value="Switch to Aristo"
      actionListener="#{currentTheme.setTheme('aristo')}"/>
  </p:column>
  <p:column>
    <p:commandButton ajax="false" value="Switch to Afterwork"
      actionListener="#{currentTheme.setTheme('afterwork')}"/>
  </p:column>
  <p:column>
    <p:commandButton ajax="false" value="Switch to Vader"
      actionListener="#{currentTheme.setTheme('vader')}"/>
  </p:column>
</p:panelGrid>
```

The `panelGrid` component lays out child components in a table. Because we used the PrimeFaces `panelGrid` component, the table and cells have a border, and each cell has a background image or color depending on the theme that is currently being used. We want to have each button laid out horizontally. Hence, we set the columns attribute with a value of 3 so that we have only one row.

The `column` tag defines the content of each cell in `panelGrid` and each `column` tag contains one `commandButton`.

The PrimeFaces `panelGrid` component, combined with the row and column tags, provides the flexibility of an HTML table, with th, tr, and td child tags and skins them with the current theme. The standard JSF `panelGrid` component is not as easily laid out. However, it is still very useful when you want a table layout without the skinning.

Each `commandButton` has a similar function, and the attributes defined are also similar. The attribute common to each button is `ajax="false"`. The PrimeFaces `commandButton` is AJAX-enabled by default. Like its JSF standard counterpart, it also submits the contents of its parent form. However, submission is performed by default by an AJAX request. We want to use a PrimeFaces `commandButton` for the theme but, because we are changing the theme using it, we need to either update the entire page using AJAX or simply perform a full POST request for the page. This will result in the page being sent in its entirety to the browser. To do this, we tell the component that it should not use AJAX.

The `value` attribute sets the label for `commandButton`, and its value should be self explanatory. The `actionListener` attribute for each `commandButton` is the most interesting because we use it to call the theme property setter method to set the theme explicitly.

Here is one of the `actionListener` attributes, which sets the theme to `vader`:

```
actionListener="#{currentTheme.setTheme('vader')}"
```

The EL expression used here calls the setter method with a string value `'vader'`, and the method is called when you click on the button as if you had a field that contained the value of `'vader'`, which would be submitted as part of the POST request. The JSF framework does make things like this very easy, and PrimeFaces leverages JSF to the fullest.

If you look at the EL Expression in `chaptersTemplate`, the theme is accessed without having to call a method. It simply references the name of the property, which is the theme in this case. This is a very powerful feature of EL because if we reference a property, the EL evaluation is context-sensitive, that is, it will call the `getter` or `setter` method, depending on the situation. If you look at the ThemeSwitcher, it has a `value` attribute with references to the `currentTheme` Bean's `theme` property. The `getter` method is called to set the currently selected theme in the session for the user, but the `setter` method is called when we change the theme to be used. We don't need to worry about which method to call though; EL does this for us as long as we use a property reference.

The one thing that we haven't specified is the page that we send the request to and respond with. This isn't specified in the `form` tag with an action attribute. So, how does JSF know which page needs to be requested?

Unless we specify the action attribute of `commandButton`, JSF assumes that we are requesting the same page and sends it in response. Because we no longer specify an action in the form, it is very easy to request a page depending on the component clicked. We can indeed even make the components action-dependent on the values submitted by calling a method that returns the page as a string, which is what we want to be sent in response.

The `actionListener` attribute of each of the `commandButton` components sets a different theme and causes the entire page to be sent to the browser.

Save the changes and then refresh the page in the browser. The following screenshot shows how things look now:

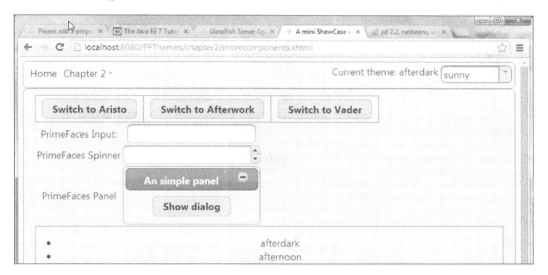

Click on one of the theme switcher buttons to see what happens. Because a complete page is requested from the server, there is a noticeable flicker in the browser, and things take much longer to complete. However, we demonstrated the ability to change themes without having to use a ThemeSwitcher component.

The real-world uses for this include being able to switch themes depending on the customer requirements for different company designs of the same application, or choosing a theme depending on the time of the day for the user.

Summary

We have now come to the end of the chapter and achieved a lot. While we pat ourselves on the shoulder or drink a well-earned cup of coffee/tea, let us review what we have done up to now.

We had a brief look at the difference between standard JSF and PrimeFaces components in terms of the HTML that is generated for them. One of the issues with standard JSF components is the lack of accessibility support. By default, PrimeFaces addresses this issue.

We added extra themes to the project and then set the appropriate context parameter in web.xml to use one of them instead of the default aristo theme. We then added code that displays the name of the current theme being used. We created two JavaBeans, which allow us to set and change the theme for each user independent of the application settings as well as provide a list of themes that a user can choose from.

In order to make things easier when adding content to the project, we created a Facelets Template, which can be used to add standard content to each of the pages, that is, a Facelets Template Client of the template. We also displayed the currently chosen theme. To top it all, we added a ThemeSwitcher component to it as well.

We then created the home page for the project as a Facelets Template Client. We also created a mini showcase for PrimeFaces components and linked this page to the template.

In the mini showcase, we also added buttons, which enabled us to change themes without using the ThemeSwitcher.

What we didn't do is change the difference.xhtml page to use chaptersTemplate. This is left as an exercise for you.

We touched on how we read and write to Bean properties using EL expressions, the way EL shields us from the complexity of whether to call a getter property method or a setter property method, and how we can explicitly set a property value.

All in all, we achieved a lot. Well done!

In the next chapter, we will look at the frameworks used to develop and use a PrimeFaces theme—jQuery, jQuery UI, and ThemeRoller.

3
jQuery UI, ThemeRoller, and the Anatomy of a Theme

Now that we have a working application, we will look at how a theme is structured. We are going to study the difference between the layout that an application uses and its look and feel. Next we will investigate how PrimeFaces uses jQuery UI to apply a theme to an application. We will then proceed to adding a new theme to the project.

In this chapter, we will cover the following topics:

- jQuery UI and its standard CSS rules
- The difference between a layout and the look and feel of an application
- How PrimeFaces uses the jQuery UI CSS rules to apply a theme to its components
- The simplest way of adjusting any theme using custom CSS rules – changing the font and initial font size
- When simple changes are not enough – introducing ThemeRoller
- Using ThemeRoller to create a theme and download it
- CSS in a custom theme as compared to a PrimeFaces theme
- Packaging a theme to make it fully compatible with PrimeFaces and adding a custom theme to a project
- How to add a new theme to ThemeSwitcher

jQuery UI and its standard CSS rules

The jQuery UI framework (for more information about this framework, visit http://jqueryui.com/) is a **jQuery Foundation project** (visit http://jquery.com/ to find out more about jQuery).

The homepage of the official site of jQuery UI states the following:

"jQuery UI is a curated set of user interface interactions, effects, widgets, and themes built on top of the jQuery JavaScript Library."

Part of the preceding quote mentions themes, and it is this facet of jQuery UI that interests us because PrimeFaces uses jQuery and the jQuery UI theme framework.

The jQuery UI themes are represented by a set of CSS rules that define the look and feel of its various components.

It is these rules that we will use to create themes.

The difference between a layout and the look and feel of UI components

jQuery UI also provides a framework to create UI components known as **widgets**, which use CSS rules to define things such as a widget's width, height, margins, padding, and the positioning of the HTML elements that they are built from.

Here is a simple example to illustrate the difference between a layout and the look and feel of a component.

A developer created a jQuery UI widget called `SimpleWidget`, which uses a `div` tag as its container.

jQuery UI uses simple naming conventions so that the widget layout CSS rules and the look and feel (theme) CSS rules remain separate. This way, you can apply different themes to the same widget without having to change the layout CSS rules that are specific to the widget itself. jQuery UI also provides a default theme that supplies sensible defaults.

The widget produces the following in HTML:

```
<div id="firstSimpleWidget" class="ui-simplewidget ui-widget ui-
    helper-reset">This is SimpleWidget in action!</div>
```

In the `div` tag, the `id` attribute is used by jQuery to identify it to set up a plugin.

The `class` attribute has several entries; some of these entries are as follows:

- `ui-simplewidget`: This is a CSS rule used by the `SimpleWidget` plugin to set how a plugin should be laid out. Therefore, this is the CSS layout rule. Note that the name of the rule contains the name of the widget in simple form, `simplewidget`.

- **ui-widget**: This is a special rule; it is a default rule from jQuery UI, but it is also defined in the look and feel, or theme, CSS file. The theme CSS rule supersedes the default UI CSS rule when the theme CSS file is loaded after the jQuery UI CSS file.

- **ui-helper-reset**: This is a rule that is used to iron out browser differences for the default values expected for block containers such as div. This rule is also part of the jQuery UI layout CSS rules.

Each PrimeFaces theme contains one CSS file in which all the CSS rules are defined. This file is called theme.css. Here are the rules defined for the UI **Darkness** theme:

```css
/* This rule sets simple dimensions for the widget container */

.ui-simplewidget {
    width: 900px;
    height: 200px;
}
/* This is the default CSS rule from jQuery UI. */

.ui-widget {
    font-family: Verdana, Arial, sans-serif;
    font-size: 1.1em;
}
/* This rule overrides the default rule and is one of the Theme CSS
rules */

.ui-widget {
    font-family: 'Segoe UI', Arial, sans-serif;
    font-size: 1.1em;
}
.ui-helper-reset {
    margin: 0;
    padding: 0;
    border: 0;
    outline: 0;
    line-height: 1.3;
    text-decoration: none;
    font-size: 100%;
    list-style: none;
}
```

The widget layout CSS rule named `ui-simplewidget` does not define anything that affects how the widget looks on the page other than its dimension.

The theme CSS rule named `ui-widget` does not define anything that affects the layout of the widget.

By separating the layout from the theme CSS rules, jQuery UI has made it easy for widget developers to create new features for their websites, while web designers can concentrate on the *look and feel* of a website by using themes.

PrimeFaces uses jQuery, jQuery UI, and themes to build components in the pages of a web application, and we can use the theme rules to create themes without worrying about the individual components or widgets.

The kind of rules that make up a theme can be classified as follows:

- **Component containers**: These rules define how the widget containers, and their headers and content look. They also define the rules for input components.
- **Interaction states**: These rules define how widgets look when they are in the `default,` `hover`, and `active` states.
- **Interaction cues**: These rules define how widgets look when highlighted/selected, for error highlighting, primary or secondary components, and for disabled components.
- **States and images**: These indicate how icons should look, similar to the interaction state rules.
- **Positioning**: These define the rules regarding where to position icons within a component.
- **Miscellaneous visuals:** These define the rules that specify corner rules.
- **Overlay and shadow**: These define the rules that specify how widgets use overlays; for example, a dialog box, its look, and the shadow it casts on the background.

How PrimeFaces uses the jQuery UI CSS rules

PrimeFaces uses the same conventions to separate the component layouts and the look and feel of the component as jQuery UI does. PrimeFaces components also use the same theme CSS rules to define how your application looks and feels on the page.

PrimeFaces components provide their own layout rules that are separate from the theme rules. So, a theme can be applied without you having to worry about changing any component-specific layout rules. Because of this, we can use the tools provided by jQuery UI to create our own themes.

Changing the initial font and font size

Before we go further with developing our own theme, it is possible to change parts of the *look and feel* without creating our own theme from scratch. Quite often, one of the standard PrimeFaces themes is very close to how we want our web application to look. Having chosen one and added it to our web app, we may decide that we need to change the font family and size.

If we open the `default.css` file (in `resources/css`) we can add the following rules:

```
/* This will be applied to all HTML in the page and not just
PrimeFaces components*/

root {
    font-size: 12px;
    font-family: 'Segoe UI', Arial, sans-serif;
}
/* We can adjust the font-size value if we wish to make PrimeFaces
   components stand out by making them larger or smaller so that
   they don't take up as much space on the page */

.ui-widget {
    font-family: 'Segoe UI', Arial, sans-serif;
    font-size: 1em;
}
.ui-widget .ui-widget {
    font-size: 1em;
}
.ui-widget input,
.ui-widget select,
.ui-widget textarea,
.ui-widget button {
    font-family: 'Segoe UI', Arial, sans-serif;
    font-size: 0.8em;
}
```

Please note that in order for the `Segoe UI` font family to be usable it must be installed on your machine.

These rules will ensure that the web app has the same font in the same size, not just for the PrimeFaces components that we use, but also for all the other text in our page.

If you do this, and then build and run your web application, you will see that the rules defined in `default.css` now override those of the PrimeFaces theme that we chose.

This happens because we have ensured that `default.css` is loaded after the PrimeFaces theme CSS file.

Using our own CSS file to define the general look and feel rules is okay, but using one to create our own theme is too unwieldy. Furthermore, this means that we lose the ability to change the theme during runtime.

Creating a theme and downloading it

In this section, we are going to use the jQuery **ThemeRoller** tool to create a custom theme, which can be downloaded and eventually added to a project.

If you visit `http://jqueryui.com/`, there are lots of links to choose from. The one that interests us is the **Themes** link highlighted in the following screenshot:

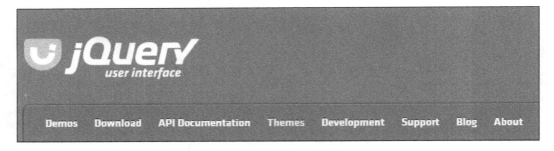

By following the link, you will come across to a page that has quite a few things going on. Most notable, for me at least, is the big **Download theme** button:

Before we use this, let us take some time to explore the page.

What we have here is a tool that allows us to change the CSS settings for the theme and see those changes reflected in the demo content immediately. Also, we do not need to know any CSS in order to change things.

We can also choose an existing theme from the **Gallery** tab and change things until we are happy with the result. Then we can use the big **Download theme** button to get the resulting theme CSS file that we want.

If we go to the **Gallery** tab, there are a variety of themes available to us. I have chosen the **Smoothness** theme. Now click on the **Roll Your Own** tab.

I decided that I want the font to be the same as the one that we defined in `default.css`. To do so, let's perform the following steps:

1. Click on **Font Settings**, and you will see something similar to the following screenshot:

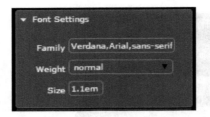

2. In the **Family** input field, change the value to `Segoe UI,Arial,sans-serif`.

3. Then change the value of the **Size** field to `1em`.

4. As we fill out the fields, we change the location of the cursor by pressing *Tab* to go to the next editable field. The changes that we make are made to the demo content to the right of the page.

If you now change the theme chosen to something else, you will see that not only does the *look and feel* of the demo content change, but also your changes are retained too!

Once you have finished creating a theme using ThemeRoller, you can then download it.

However, before you do that, create a bookmark for the page because all the values that we changed are also passed as a set of parameters to the page.

By doing this, we can come back to our theme without having to remember everything that we changed before. By clicking on the **Download theme** button, you will come to a page with rather a lot of choices to make.

 At the time of writing this book, PrimeFaces uses jQuery UI version 1.10.4, so choose this at the top of the page.

As we are not using any jQuery UI components, PrimeFaces provides those for us. We can simply keep the **Toggle All** option in **Components** off. The checkbox for this is just below the **Version** choices.

At the bottom of the page, there is a checkbox that should read **Custom Theme**. If it doesn't and you want to simply download one from the **Gallery** tab, choose one.

Below this, there is a field where you can give your theme a name. We don't want to change this field because we are going to use another tool to convert the ThemeRoller-generated ZIP file into a PrimeFaces theme that is ready for use in a web application. You can leave the **CSS Scope** field empty.

Now click on **Download** and save the file in a convenient location. The file should be named `jquery-ui-1.10.4.custom.zip`.

Comparing our theme to a PrimeFaces one

If you look at the rules in the theme that we generated and compare them to a PrimeFaces one, you will see that we have exactly the same set of rules in both. Although we have the same set of rules, it is their definitions that determine how a theme looks and feels.

In order to view the CSS rules in our theme, we need to unpack the ZIP file that we downloaded. We then need to navigate our way through the folders until we see one called `custom-theme`. This folder contains two versions of the same CSS file—a human-readable version and one that has been minimized to reduce the file's size.

The following screenshot shows the path that you need to take to open the CSS files:

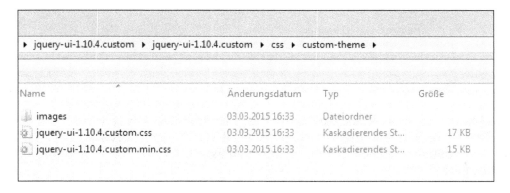

In order to view the CSS of a PrimeFaces theme, you can unpack one of the themes that PrimeFaces supplies and search for a `theme.css` file, download one of the pre-made themes of the same name from ThemeRoller, or unpack the pre-made theme in exactly the same way as we did for the custom theme.

Packaging and adding our custom theme to the project

First of all, we need to create a JAR file that PrimeFaces will accept as a valid theme. Fortunately, a very kind PrimeFaces contributor provided us with a tool that will take the ZIP file from ThemeRoller and convert it into a PrimeFaces-ready theme JAR. Go to `https://themeroller.osnode.com/themeroller/` and follow the instructions there:

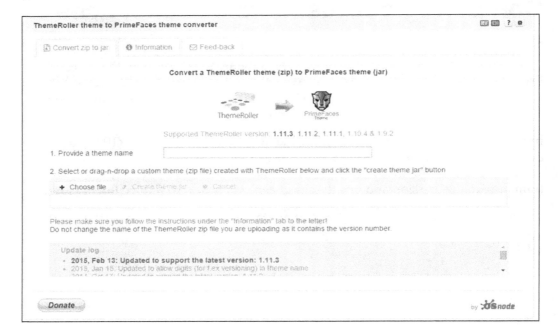

The JAR file that was created can be used in your PrimeFaces-based web apps now. But first, we need to add the JAR file to the local Maven repository before we can add it as a dependency to our project. Maven makes this easy. For more information on this, visit `http://maven.apache.org/guides/mini/guide-3rd-party-jars-local.html`.

In the following example, I used the following Maven command to get Maven to install the **Moodyblue** theme's JAR file into my local repository.

For the example to work, you need to be in the same folder as the JAR file. For your theme, you should change the file and the `groupId` and `artifactId` values appropriately:

```
mvn install:install-file -Dfile=moodyblue.jar -
   DgroupId=org.pfthemes -DartifactId=moodyblue -Dversion=1.0.10 -
   Dpackaging=jar
```

Once this is done, you can add the theme file to your project as a Maven dependency by referencing its `groupId`, `artifactId`, and `version` parameters when you add the dependency.

In *Chapter 2, Introducing PrimeFaces Themes*, we set the theme the application uses by setting a context parameter in the web application's `web.xml` file.

We can quickly test the new theme by simply changing the following part of `web.xml` to; in this case, simply `moodyblue` and restart the web application:

```
<context-param>
<param-name>primefaces.THEME</param-name>
<param-value>moodyblue</param-value>
</context-param>
```

Adding the new theme to the ThemeSwitcher class

If you open the **ThemeSwitcher** class in the IDE, you can simply add the name of your theme to the list of themes that are available for you to choose:

```
private final String[] themes = {"afterdark",
    "afternoon",
    "afterwork",
    "aristo",
    "black-tie",
    "blitzer",
    "bluesky",
    "bootstrap",
```

```
    "casablanca",
    "cupertino",
    "cruze",
    "dark-hive",
    "delta",
    "dot-luv",
    "eggplant",
    "excite-bike",
    "flick",
    "glass-x",
    "home",
    "hot-sneaks",
    "humanity",
    "le-frog",
    "midnight",
    "mint-choc",
    "moodyblue",
    "overcast",
    "pepper-grinder",
    "redmond",
    "rocket",
    "sam",
    "smoothness",
    "south-street",
    "start",
    "sunny",
    "swanky-purse",
    "trontastic",
    "ui-darkness",
    "ui-lightness",
    "vader"};
```

We will need to revert the changes that we just made to the `web.xml` file. If the file is still open, then simply use **Undo** in the editor. You can also use the IDE **local history** feature:

```
<context-param>
<param-name>primefaces.THEME</param-name>
<param-value>#{currentTheme.theme}</param-value>
</context-param>
```

Now clean and build the project before running it. You will see that you can now select your new theme in ThemeSwitcher.

Summary

In this chapter, we have covered the difference between a layout and the look and feel of CSS. It is now clear as to why the separation of the two types of CSS is a good idea. We have also looked at jQuery UI ThemeRoller and used it to create our own theme. Having done this, we then used the **OSnode** (short for **Open Source node**) ThemeRoller in the PrimeFaces theme converter to create a PrimeFaces-ready theme. We have used Maven to add the new theme JAR to our local Maven repository and have then added it as a dependency to our project. We have tested the theme before adding it to the list of available themes in ThemeSwitcher.

In the next chapter, we will look in detail at how a theme actually works by comparing the HTML generated by a standard JSF `inputText` component and a PrimeFaces `inputText` component.

4
A PrimeFaces inputText Component in Detail

In this chapter, we are going to take a simple UI component and use browser developer tools to examine and change the CSS rules applied to it. We will strip away some of the mysteries involved in applying a theme to your application.

In addition to this, we will see that PrimeFaces applies theme rules dynamically. We will learn how to do this for a standard JSF component too.

In this chapter, we will cover the following topics:

- Creating a new JSF page and adding a standard inputText component
- Examining the UI element using the browser developer tool
- Adding a PrimeFaces inputText component to the page and comparing these two elements
- Adding CSS classes to the standard inputText field to make it look like a PrimeFaces inputText field

Creating a new JSF page and adding a standard inputText component

In this section, we will use an **Integrated Development Environment** (IDE) to create a new folder and add some pages into it, as follows:

1. In your web project, create a new folder in the webapp project folder and call it chapter4.

2. Then create three JSF template client pages based on the `chaptersTemplate.xhtml` template in the new folder and call them `index.xhtml`, `withPFEquivalent.xhtml,` and `standardJSFWithPFThemes.xhtml.`

3. In the `chaptersTemplate.xhtml` template, add the following code under the `chapter2` submenu:

```
<p:submenu id="chapter4" label="Chapter 4">
  <p:menuitem id="c4index" value="Standard JSF inputText"
    url="/chapter4/index.xhtml"/>
  <p:menuitem id="c4andPFInput" value="Standard JSF vs
    PrimeFaces inputText" url="/chapter4/
    withPFEquivalent.xhtml"/>
  <p:menuitem id="c4standardWithPFThemes" value="Standard
    inputText with PrimeFaces theme" url="/chapter4/
    standardJSFWithPFThemes.xhtml"/>
</p:submenu>
```

4. Now open `chapter4/index.html` and replace everything inside the `ui:composition` tag with the following:

```
<ui:define name="title">
  PrimeFaces Themes Development Chapter 4
</ui:define>
<ui:define name="content">
  <h1>A standard JSF inputText component</h1>
  <h:form id="mainForm">
    <h:panelGrid columns="2">
      <h:outputLabel value="Standard JSF Input: "/>
      <h:inputText/>
    </h:panelGrid>
  </h:form>
</ui:define>
```

5. You will need to add the `xmlns:h=http://xmlns.jcp.org/jsf/html` namespace to the page.

 The `ui:composition` tag has a namespace already added.

6. If you start the application, you will see the start page with the new submenu that we just added, which looks like the following screenshot:

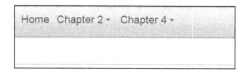

7. Open the **Chapter 4** menu and click on the **Standard JSF inputText** item.

8. The page that opens looks similar to the following screenshot:

The box to the right of the **Standard JSF Input**: label is a simple input text field; nothing surprising about that. When you change the theme, you will also see that the *look and feel* of the box does not change. The following screenshot shows the page using the **afternoon** theme. As you can see, the input text is still just a box:

Examining the UI element using the browser developer tool

Modern browsers come with tools or extensions, which can be used by web developers to see *under the hood* of a page. As we want to examine the HTML that a JSF inputText component produces, or *renders* (in JSF terms), we use the developer tools to view the actual HTML produced in the page.

I used Google Chrome for this book, but those of you who use Firefox will have the same standard tools available. The good news for those of you who use Internet Explorer is that version 11 also has a set of developer tools similar to those available in Google Chrome and Firefox.

In order to view the code, we don't right-click on the page and click on **View code source** anymore. If you do so now, you will see a simple page containing the text version of the HTML that was rendered. This is hard to read and often not formatted for us to read easily. What we actually do is place the cursor of the mouse over an element on the page, which is the input text in this case, right-click on it, and click on **Inspect element**.

By default, this opens a panel at the bottom of the page and displays something similar to the following screenshot:

The highlighted HTML for the input text looks very simple and is indeed pretty much how you would add an input text element by hand. The `name` attribute for the input field is automatically generated by JSF because we didn't specify an ID attribute for the `h:inputText` component. Other than this, it doesn't look like JSF does anything special.

Adding a PrimeFaces inputText component to the page and comparing these two elements

Now we are going to add a PrimeFaces `inputText` component to the `withPFEquivalent.xhtml` page and then use the browser developer tool to compare the rendered HTML using the following steps:

1. Open the `withPFEquivalent.xhtml` page and replace the existing HTML inside the `ui:composition` tag with the following:

```
<ui:define name="title">
  PrimeFaces Themes Development Chapter 4
</ui:define>
<ui:define name="content">
  <h1>A standard JSF inputText component vs a PrimeFaces
    inputText</h1>
  <h:form id="mainForm">
    <h:panelGrid columns="2">
      <h:outputLabel value="Standard JSF Input: "/>
      <h:inputText/>
      <h:outputLabel value="PrimeFaces Input:"/>
      <p:inputText/>
    </h:panelGrid>
  </h:form>
</ui:define>
```

2. After saving the changes, we then navigate to **Chapter 4 | Standard JSF vs PrimeFaces inputText**. The page that opens looks similar to the following screenshot:

The PrimeFaces input text stands out compared to the standard one as it has rounded corners, and a shadow effect gives it a three-dimensional *look and feel*. This is what the PrimeFaces theme does, and changing the theme will change how the PrimeFaces input text component looks. If we change the theme to **bootstrap**, we will see what's shown in the following screenshot:

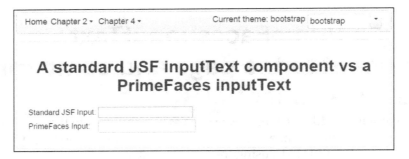

Note how the standard input text stays the same and the PrimeFaces input text changes.

We are now going to examine the rendered HTML of both input text components and compare them using the browser development tool.
Place the mouse cursor in the PrimeFaces input text, right-click on it, and click on **Inspect element**. The developer panel opens, and you will see what's shown in the following screenshot:

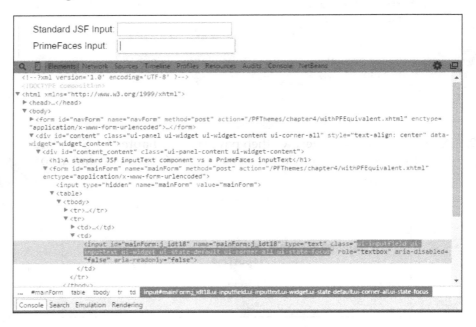

It is immediately clear that the HTML for the PrimeFaces input text has a lot more attributes set. The `class` attribute values for the HTML input are highlighted to show that the PrimeFaces `p:inputText` attribute uses both jQuery UI layout CSS rules (`ui-inputfield` and `ui-inputtext`) and jQuery UI theme CSS rules (`ui-widget`, `ui-state-default`, `ui-corner-all`, and `ui-state-focus`). The **Accessible Rich Internet Applications (ARIA)** attributes are also set, so this component is compatible with the ARIA accessibility standard too. PrimeFaces sets the ID as well as the name of the HTML component, something which the standard JSF does not do unless you set the `id` attribute in the tag.

Now, let us compare the two HTML tags:

- For the standard input text the HTML tag is as follows:

  ```
  <input type="text" name="mainForm:j_idt16">
  ```

- For the PrimeFaces input text the HTML tag is as follows:

  ```
  <input id="mainForm:j_idt18" name="mainForm:j_idt18"
    type="text" class="ui-inputfield ui-inputtext ui-widget
    ui-state-default ui-corner-all" role="textbox" aria-
    disabled="false" aria-readonly="false">
  ```

The differences are clear, and the effect the applied CSS rules have to the way the input text looks is also obvious. The nice thing about how PrimeFaces uses the jQuery UI is that it makes it simple to make the components look nice on the page and to use a set of standard CSS rules to do so. Changing the theme only changes what those CSS rules mean, but not the names of those rules.

Seeing how simple things are, it should then be possible to make the standard input text look the same as the PrimeFaces input text.

Turning a standard component into a PrimeFaces one

At least as far as its looks are concerned...

We are now going to try and use the same CSS rules that the PrimeFaces input text uses for the standard one, as follows:

1. Rather than changing the `withPFEquivalent.xhtml` page, open the `standardJSFWithPFThemes.xhtml` page and replace the code inside the `ui:composition` tag with the same code from the `withPFEquivalent.xhtml` page.

2. Then edit the `h:inputText` tag so that it looks like this:

```
<h:inputText class="ui-inputfield ui-inputtext ui-widget
    ui-state-default ui-corner-all ui-state-focus"/>
```

3. Reload the page. You will now see that the standard input text looks like the PrimeFaces text. However, there is one glaring difference—the standard input text does not have focus and it has a nice glow around it. The PrimeFaces input text does not have focus either, but the glow is absent. The following screenshot shows the difference:

```
Standard JSF Input: [                    ]
PrimeFaces Input:   [                    ]
```

If you look at the CSS rules for the PrimeFaces input text by inspecting it in the page, you will see that we have one CSS rule too many. The `ui-state-focus` rule is not in the list of rules set in the `class` attribute of the element. If you look back at the screenshot showing the code for the PrimeFaces input text element and then look where the mouse cursor is, you will see that the PrimeFaces input text has focus and the same glow effect that we see in the preceding screenshot. The difference is that without focus, the PrimeFaces input text does not use the `ui-state-focus` CSS rule.

Before what is happening is explained, first remove the `ui-state-focus` CSS rule from the standard input text class attribute and compare it to the PrimeFaces one.

After refreshing the page, you will see that both input text components look the same. You have successfully applied the theme CSS rules to your standard component to make it look like the PrimeFaces one. If you now change the theme, you will see that your standard component's appearance also changes.

Now compare what happens when the standard component receives focus to when the PrimeFaces component receives it.

The appearance of the PrimeFaces component changes when it receives focus, but the standard one does not! This also happens when we hover the mouse cursor over the PrimeFaces component.

What is happening is that PrimeFaces provides feedback to the user as to which input component is currently active or when the mouse cursor is over it. This is a very important facet of UI design that improves the user experience by aiding to orient the user as to where they currently are on the page. Normally, this would require a lot of clever JavaScript and CSS rules for you to achieve this by using the standard JSF components. PrimeFaces does all this for us, and how the components look depending on their state is also part of the theme. We see no JavaScript in the rendered HTML for the tag because PrimeFaces uses jQuery to bind the dynamic behavior in the page.

In a simplified form, we will now do the same.

Edit the h:inputText tag so that it looks like the following code snippet. The code that needs to be added is in bold:

```
<h:inputText class="ui-inputfield ui-inputtext ui-widget ui-state-
    default ui-corner-all"
    onfocus="$(this).toggleClass('ui-state-hover').toggleClass('ui-
        state-focus')"
    onmouseover="$(this).toggleClass('ui-state-hover')"
    onblur="$(this).toggleClass('ui-state-hover').toggleClass('ui-
        state-focus')"/>
```

If you are not familiar with jQuery, then the JavaScript may look a little alien to you. It is definitely worth your while visiting the jQuery web site at http://jquery.com/ and learning how this amazing library works.

What we have done is bind small jQuery event handlers to the input text so that the CSS rules are added or removed depending on what the mouse is doing. If you refresh the page now, you will see that your standard input text now behaves very much like the PrimeFaces one when you hover the mouse cursor over it or give the component focus.

It was a lot of hard work to achieve the same *look and feel* for the standard components as that of the PrimeFaces components. Now, imagine how much work would be needed to transform all the standard JSF components in a similar manner! Fortunately, PrimeFaces doesn't just provide components equivalent to the standard JSF ones, it provides many more besides. The input text component is also the simplest of all the input components available.

Summary

We have learned how a basic JSF standard component's HTML looks compared to the PrimeFaces rendered code. We have also seen how PrimeFaces uses theme CSS rules to provide a standard *look and feel* for its components. Lastly, we have learned that although we can mimic this for standard JSF components, it requires a lot of hard work on our part.

In the next chapter, we are going to tweak our custom theme so that it provides us with exactly the *look and feel* that we desire.

5
Let's Get Creative

In this chapter, we are going to build on the work that we did in the previous chapter by using our custom theme and tweaking it according to our needs. This will expose some of the weaknesses of ThemeRoller-generated themes, and we'll learn how to compensate for them.

A very useful breakdown of the types of rules that jQuery UI defines is given at `https://api.jqueryui.com/theming/css-framework/`.

We'll cover the following topics in this chapter:

- Creating a new JSF page
- Using your unpackaged theme and applying it to your application
- Changing the initial font and font size in your theme
- Changing the foreground and background colors
- Changing the highlighted, active, and selected CSS rules
- Changing the rounding rules
- Changing the shadow effects
- Changing the menu's background

Creating a new JSF page

We will first create a new folder in web pages called `chapter5`, as this has become a standard practice for new chapters. Then, we create a new JSF template client called `index.xhtml` and add a link to it in the `chaptersTemplate` template file. When adding a submenu, use `Chapter 5` for the label, and for the menu item, use `Let's get creative!` for its value.

In the title section, replace the text title with the title of this chapter, Let's get creative!.

In the content section, replace the text content with the following code:

```
<p:button value="This is a button"/>
<p:panel header="This is the panel header" toggleable="true"
toggleTitle="Click me to open/close the panel">
  <h:panelGrid columns="1">
    <h:outputText value="Here is some panel content"/>
  </h:panelGrid>
</p:panel>
```

Now, run the application and navigate to the newly created page. You will see the PrimeFaces **Panel** component, which is shown in the following screenshot:

The PrimeFaces **Panel** component uses theme CSS rules for the widget header, widget content and the dynamic state rules and is simple enough that we can concentrate on altering the rules without having to delve into how the component is laid out.

Using your unpackaged theme and applying it to your application

In *Chapter 3, jQuery UI, ThemeRoller, and the Anatomy of a Theme*, we created a custom theme and packaged it using the **OSNode** theme packaging tool. In this chapter, we are going to need the original CSS file and images folder from the ThemeRoller custom theme that we downloaded and to add it into our project.

By adding the CSS file and folder, we will be able to easily change the CSS rules and immediately see the changes that were made to our theme in the web project.

Go to the folder with the original downloaded zip file in it. I renamed my zip file moodyblue.zip because that is the name of my theme, which is why we see the name moodyblue in some of the screenshots.

We will need to unzip the file into the same folder and then locate the css folder, as shown in the following screenshot:

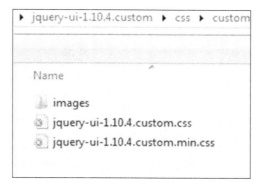

In the web project under Web Pages/resources, we need to create a new folder named primefaces-<ourtheme>2. The <ourtheme> part needs to be changed to the name used for our theme. In my case, this is moodyblue, which results in the creation of a new folder named primefaces-moodyblue2.

Now, you need to copy the images folder and the jquery-ui-1.10.4.custom.css file into the folder that we just created. Then, rename the CSS file theme.css. The name of the folder and the CSS file are required by PrimeFaces so that it can treat our theme in exactly the same way as it does its own themes.

If, for some reason, the changes are not made correctly, then the images will not be displayed. If this happens, you will need to check and possibly correct any errors. CSS tends to fail silently. So, there will be no other indication of a possible error.

In order to complete the manual packaging, we need to edit the theme.css file in the following manner:

1. We need to search for and replace all the instances of url(" with url("#{resource['primefaces-<ourtheme>2:, where <ourtheme> is replaced with our theme name, which is moodyblue in my case. So, url(" is replaced with url("#{resource['primefaces-moodyblue2:.

2. We need to search and replace all the instances of .png with .png'] }.

To make the result of the changes clear, here is one of the CSS rules before and after the changes:

1. The CSS rule before changes:

```css
.ui-widget-content {
  border: 1px solid #aaaaff;
  background: #ffffff url("images/ui-
  bg_flat_75_ffffff_40x100.png") 50% 50% repeat-x;
  color: #222222;
}
```

2. The CSS rule after changes:

```css
.ui-widget-content {
  border: 1px solid #aaaaff;
  background: #ffffff url("#{resource['primefaces-
  moodyblue2:images/ui-bg_flat_75_ffffff_40x100.png']}")
  50% 50% repeat-x;
  color: #222222;
}
```

The reason why you need to change the CSS rules that access resources using the `url` accessor is because JSF requires that resources are accessed using the Resource Manager. If you don't do this, then the Resource Manager will not be able to access them and they will not be made available to your web application.

Fortunately, these are all the changes that you need to make to the `theme.css` file.

You can now add the name of this theme to the list of themes in the `ThemeService` class as you did in *Chapter 3, jQuery UI, ThemeRoller, and the Anatomy of a Theme*, so that you can access it using the ThemeSwitcher in your app.

If you build and run your application, you can now change the theme being used to the one you just added. In my case, that is `moodyblue2`. The homepage of the application now appears as shown in the following screenshot:

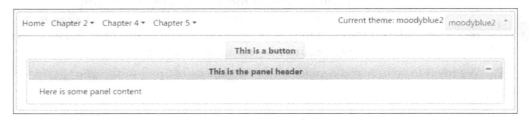

For the rest of the chapter, we will look at and change various CSS rules that make up parts of a theme.

Changing the initial font and font size in your theme

One of the first things that a website owner specifies is the font, or fonts, that they want to use in their website. Together with the logo and the foreground and background colors, these are generally the things that they want their visitors to see.

Changing the font characteristics of your theme is also the easiest place to start.

First, locate the CSS rules that set the font family. We open the `theme.css` file and search for `font-family`. My editor shows that this is defined by just two rules — `ui-widget` and `ui-widget button`.

In `moodyblue2`, the rules look like this:

```
.ui-widget {
    font-family: 'Segoe UI',Arial,sans-serif;
    font-size: 1.0em;
}
.ui-widget input,
.ui-widget select,
.ui-widget textarea,
.ui-widget button {
  font-family: 'Segoe UI',Arial,sans-serif;
}
```

Both the rules define the same font family, with the first choice of font being Segoe UI. This font is incidentally the one that Windows 7 uses as its system font. I chose it because it is a very good font to use in a digital environment, as it has simple and clear lines and is familiar to a great many people.

Let's experiment a little. What happens if we change `ui-widget font-family`?

We simply remove the `'Segoe UI',` part of the rule and then save and refresh the page.

[NetBeans automatically refreshes the page when you save changes.]

The changes are shown in the following screenshot:

The changes are subtle because the Arial and Segoe UI fonts are closely related, but they are there. We changed the `font-family` attribute of all the PrimeFaces components and the content that they contain, with the exception of the button above the panel. In fact, the second rule defines the `font-family` attribute used in the `input`, `select`, and `textarea` components as well as the buttons.

We can check this by inspecting the `"Here is some panel content"` element, selecting the **Computed** style tab, and unchecking the **Show inherited properties** checkbox, as shown in the following screenshot:

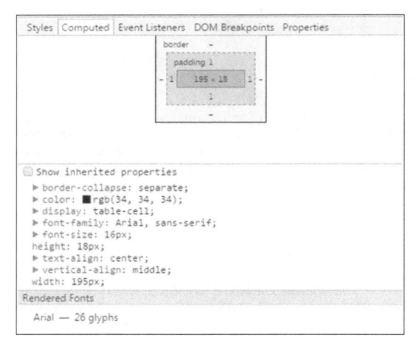

You will see that the **Rendered Fonts** section is **Arial**. So, the changes that we made worked for the content, and we can assume that this is true for all the other widgets except for buttons, which we can check in exactly the same way by examining the PrimeFaces button component. The button component uses Segoe UI, as shown in the following screenshot:

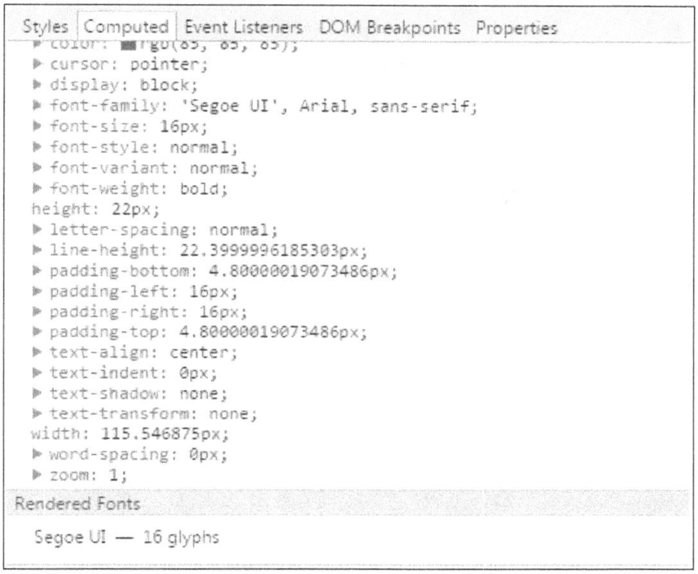

A question that you may ask here is, why do we have a separate rule for input, select, textarea, and button?

The answer is that these classes of component are so common and easily identifiable that they are often styled to make this stand out. In order to make this easier, the developers of jQuery UI provide a rule for the creation of the theme of these components so that they have a common and consistent look and feel to them. Note that we can create separate rules for each component type to make them standout from each other, if required.

We can change the `font-family` attribute of the second rule to `Times New Roman` to exaggerate the effect. If you do this, then the page will look like the following screenshot:

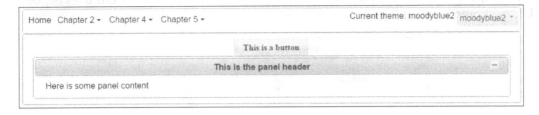

This shows why Times New Roman is never used as a general font in web applications.

Now, we will change the `font-size` attribute used.

The choice of the `font-size` attribute is made depending on how much content we want to display on a page without having the browser grow scroll bars. If we only have a small amount of content, we can use a larger `font-size` attribute. Conversely, if we have quite a lot of content to display, we choose a smaller `font-size` attribute. The larger the font, the easier it is to read. So, the choice is quite important.

For our purposes, we are initially going to use a smaller `font-size` attribute. But first, we need to find the CSS rules that define the `font-size` attribute for our theme.

As before, we search the `theme.css` file for all the instances of `font-size` and check whether we again have two CSS rules that define it, as follows:

```
.ui-widget {
  font-family: Arial,sans-serif;
  font-size: 1.0em;
}

.ui-widget .ui-widget {
  font-size: 1.0em;
}
```

They both define the `font-size` attribute for `ui-widget`, but the second rule says that all the `ui-widget` components are contained within a `ui-widget` component.

If you change the `font-size` attribute of the first rule to `0.5em` and save the file that our theme creates, the page will look similar to the following screenshot:

Everything has changed size even though we have not changed the second rule.

The following screenshot shows what happens if we redo the changes to the first rule and change the `font-size` attribute of the second rule from `1.0 em` to `smaller`:

The changes that we made to the first rule changed the `font-size` attribute for the entire page, including the `ui-widget` components inside the `ui-widget` components. The question here is, why aren't the `ui-widget` components inside the `ui-widget` components being displayed with the defined `font-size` attribute of `1.0em`? This seems counter-intuitive at first, but the answer is that because the `ui-widget` rule is more strongly associated with all the `ui-widget` components than the `ui-widget ui-widget` rule, all the `ui-widget` components are displayed with a `font-size` attribute of `0.5em`.

The second screenshot shows the effect of setting the `font-size` attribute to `smaller`. Any `ui-widget` component that is inside another `ui-widget` component is displayed with a `font-size` attribute smaller than its parent. The difference can most easily be seen in the menu panel that is opened under the `Chapter 5` menu. The text of the menu item is smaller than its parent.

This can be used to give visual clues as to the hierarchy of components and is a very useful way to show things such as menu panels, which tend to contain a lot more content than the menu when shown.

In order to use these rules in the best possible way, set an absolute value for the `font-size` attribute in the first rule and a relative value for the `font-size` attribute in the second rule.

To recap what we have learned up till now:

- We have simple rules to set the font family and size for our theme, but these rules are very powerful and need to be used correctly in order to achieve the desired effect
- We have the ability to create rules for different classes of ui components in order to make them stand out from each other
- We can use relative font sizing to make component hierarchies visibly obvious to the user

Changing the foreground and background colors

Although we have set the foreground and background color for our theme, we might want to make some changes for specific regions of a page for visual clarity.

To get started, search for color in theme.css. In order to find just color and not background-color as well, start your filter with a space character.

I found 15 instances of color. So I have to check to see which rules are of immediate interest to me. I am interested in the rules that define the look and feel of components that are not involved in the dynamic state feedback, such as any rule that defines selected, active, and hover.

This leaves us with the following four rules.

```
.ui-widget-content {
  border: 1px solid #aaaaff;
  background: #ffffff url("#{resource['primefaces-
  moodyblue2:images/ui-bg_flat_75_ffffff_40x100.png']}") 50% 50%
  repeat-x;
  color: #222222;
}
.ui-widget-content a {
  color: #222222;
}
.ui-widget-header {
  border: 1px solid #aaaaff;
  background: #ccccff url("#{resource['primefaces-
  moodyblue2:images/ui-bg_highlight-
  soft_75_ccccff_1x100.png']}") 50% 50% repeat-x;
  color: #2222ff;
```

```
    font-weight: bold;
}
.ui-widget-header a {
    color: #2222ff;
}
```

The first rule defines the look and feel for the content of a widget. In our panel, we have some text. So, it will be reasonable to assume that changing the value of `color` from `#222222` to `yellow` will cause the text to be displayed in yellow, as shown in the following screenshot:

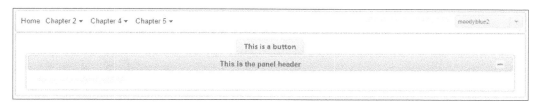

This is indeed the case. You will also see that the text `Current theme: moodyblue2` is also displayed in yellow, which is perhaps not what we wanted. The choice of yellow was made to make the effect very obvious. It also shows that the rule that we changed is also very powerful and it changes the look and feel of the entire content in the content part of a widget.

The yellow label displaying the current theme also highlights a problem with the template. The text is aligned with the top of the ThemeSwitcher, which doesn't look good. Before we go back to our content rule, we will now change the current theme's label.

Open the `chaptersTemplate.xhtml` file and search for `Current theme`.

Consider the following code:

```
<h:outputText value="Current theme: " style="vertical-align:
    top;"/>
<h:outputText value="#{currentTheme.theme} " style="vertical-
    align: top;"/>
```

The preceding code should be replaced with the following code:

```
<p:outputLabel value="Current theme: #{currentTheme.theme} "
for="themeSwitcher" style="vertical-align: 50%"/>
```

Lastly, we will create a new rule in `theme.css`. Put the following code under the rule that we just changed:

```
label.ui-outputlabel {
    color:#222222;
}
```

After saving our changes, we can see the effect on our page, as shown in the following screenshot:

The changes that you made ensure that any label that has the `.ui-outputlabel` class displays content with the `color: #222222` attribute.

When you open the ThemeSwitcher list box, you will see that all the unselected theme names are also displayed in yellow. So, there is a lot more to this than meets the eye. We have a lot of widgets that have a content component. The rule that we changed really does affect them all. Rather than worry about the `color` attribute, we display different widget content in we really should change the `color` attribute we chose. Hence, we change yellow to black and save `theme.css`. This not only looks better, but also demonstrates what happens when you use a light color with a light background `color` attribute—things become unreadable.

If you now examine the page, you will see that there are differences between the text shown in a button and that of the panel header. Quite often, we want to ensure that our theme is consistent in its look and feel.

Components such as `button` can also be highlighted with dynamic visual cues, and we want to have these consistent with other components such as the panel header.

To achieve this, we need to change the following rule:

```
.ui-state-default,
.ui-widget-content .ui-state-default,
.ui-widget-header .ui-state-default {
    border: 1px solid #d3d3ff;
```

```
background: #e6e6ff url("#{resource['primefaces-
   moodyblue2:images/ui-bg_highlight-
   hard_75_e6e6ff_1x100.png']}") 50% 50% repeat-x;
font-weight: bold;
color: #222222;
}
```

First, we change the `color` attribute to `#2222ff` and then we comment out the background definition so that it looks like this:

```
.ui-state-default,
.ui-widget-content .ui-state-default,
.ui-widget-header .ui-state-default {
  border: 1px solid #d3d3ff;
  /*    background: #e6e6ff url("#{resource['primefaces-
     moodyblue2:images/ui-bg_highlight-
     hard_75_e6e6ff_1x100.png']}") 50% 50% repeat-x; */
  font-weight: bold;
  color: #2222ff;
}
```

Then we copy the background definition from the `.ui-widget-header` rule and paste it under the background definition that we commented out.

The rule should now look like this:

```
.ui-state-default,
.ui-widget-content .ui-state-default,
.ui-widget-header .ui-state-default {
  border: 1px solid #d3d3ff;
  /*    background: #e6e6ff url("#{resource['primefaces-
     moodyblue2:images/ui-bg_highlight-
     hard_75_e6e6ff_1x100.png']}") 50% 50% repeat-x; */
  background: #ccccff url("#{resource['primefaces-
     moodyblue2:images/ui-bg_highlight-
     soft_75_ccccff_1x100.png']}") 50% 50% repeat-x;
  font-weight: bold;
  color: #2222ff;
}
```

The changes that we made cause the page to look like the following screenshot:

As you can see, our panel header and button now have a more normal look and feel. If you go back and look at the changes you made to the background definition, you will see that the background has both a `color` attribute and an image definition. The background image is defined with the `url` keyword. So with one definition, we changed both the background color and image. We could have split this up into separate `background-image` and `background-color` definitions, but CSS allows us to define one rule for the entire background. CSS has quite a few amalgamated rules that we can define, which allows us to create concise CSS files.

Changing the highlighted, active, and selected CSS rules

We are now going to examine the rules that define the dynamic visual cues. These cues are added by PrimeFaces to elements that can be highlighted, activated (when you click on them), and selected.

The following screenshot shows a menu that is highlighted:

The `Chapter 2` menu is highlighted above its drop-down menu list. The gray background is nice enough, but it doesn't fit in with the blue theme. Therefore, we are going to change it. The same highlighted effect can be seen if you `hover` your mouse over the button.

So, we need to change the rules that define how components look when the mouse hovers over them. On searching for `hover` in `theme.css`, we find two definitions that we need to look for. The definitions are for a total of 14 rules, 6 of these define how components look and 8 of them define how anchors or links look.

The first definition looks like this:

```
.ui-state-hover,
.ui-widget-content .ui-state-hover,
.ui-widget-header .ui-state-hover,
.ui-state-focus,
.ui-widget-content .ui-state-focus,
.ui-widget-header .ui-state-focus {
  border: 1px solid #9999ff;
  background: #dadada url("#{resource['primefaces-
    moodyblue2:images/ui-bg_highlight-
    hard_75_dadada_1x100.png']}") 50% 50% repeat-x;
  font-weight: bold;
  color: #212121;
}
```

We want to change the `color` and `background` attributes like we did in the last section. We first change the `color` attribute from `#212121` to `#2222ff`.

Then we copy the background definition that we commented out in the `.ui-default` rule from the last section and replace the `background` definition with it.

The rule now looks like this:

```
.ui-state-hover,
.ui-widget-content .ui-state-hover,
.ui-widget-header .ui-state-hover,
.ui-state-focus,
.ui-widget-content .ui-state-focus,
.ui-widget-header .ui-state-focus {
  border: 1px solid #9999ff;
  background: #e6e6ff url("#{resource['primefaces-
    moodyblue2:images/ui-bg_highlight-
    hard_75_e6e6ff_1x100.png']}") 50% 50% repeat-x;
  font-weight: bold;
  color: #2222ff;
}
```

We can see how the changes that we made look in the following screenshot:

I decided not to change the rules that define how links look when a person hovers a mouse over them, as I am happy with the way they look.

Incidentally, the rules that we changed define how things look when you hover a mouse over them as well as how components look when they are focused on. Components that receive focus are generally the input components. The following screenshot shows how the Mini Showcase page now looks when the PrimeFaces `inputText` component are focused on:

Because of the way the CSS rules for a theme are grouped, it is very easy to make wholesale changes. You can simply change the definition for the rules that are grouped together. It is also very easy to create separate rules to define how an input text field looks when it needs to have its own distinct look and feel.

The rules that we are going to look at in this section are those that define how a component looks when it is selected.

Fortunately, the ThemeSelector provides us with a component that is selected — the currently selected theme. The following screenshot shows how this looks:

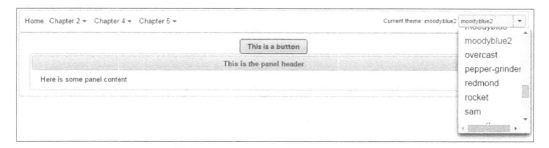

When you look very carefully at the selected theme (moodyblue2), you can just about make out that the background is different. We obviously want to make the highlighted components stand out better.

If you search for highlight in theme.css, you will find two sets of rules. The first set of rules, which are as follows, are the ones that interest us the most here:

```
.ui-state-highlight,
.ui-widget-content .ui-state-highlight,
.ui-widget-header .ui-state-highlight {
  border: 1px solid #fcefa1;
  background: #fbf9ee url("#{resource['primefaces-
    moodyblue2:images/ui-bg_highlight-
    hard_55_fbf9ee_1x100.png']}") 50% top repeat-x;
  color: #363636;
}
```

We can use the grey background from the hover rules that we changed earlier, as follows:

```
.ui-state-highlight,
.ui-widget-content .ui-state-highlight,
.ui-widget-header .ui-state-highlight {
  border: 1px solid #fcefa1;
  /*    background: #fbf9ee url("#{resource['primefaces-
    moodyblue2:images/ui-bg_highlight-
    hard_55_fbf9ee_1x100.png']}") 50% top repeat-x; */
  background: #dadada url("#{resource['primefaces-
    moodyblue2:images/ui-bg_highlight-hard_75_dadada_1x100.png']}")
    50% 50% repeat-x;
  color: #363636;
}
```

You can see how the selection now looks in the following screenshot:

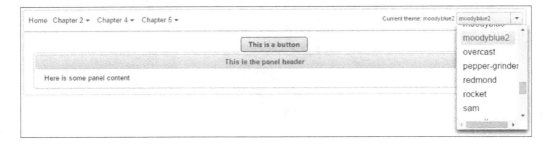

The selected item now stands out a lot more, which is what we want.

Changing the rounding rules

In this section, we are going to look at the rules that define how the corners of components are rounded.

If you search for the word "corner" in `theme.css`, you will find the `/* Corner radius */` comment. Under this comment, you will see a set of four rules that can be used to set corners.

There is one rule that is common to all — `.ui-corner-all`. The other rules specify how the top-left, top-right, bottom-left, and bottom-right corners should look.

The arrangement of rules in this way means that we can change each corner independently without having to change which rule the component or component part actually uses.

If you decide that the top-left corner should have no rounding at all, you can simply change the first rule, which initially looks like this:

```
.ui-corner-all,
.ui-corner-top,
.ui-corner-left,
.ui-corner-tl {
  border-top-left-radius: 4px;
}
```

The preceding rule can be changed to the following:

```
.ui-corner-all,
.ui-corner-top,
.ui-corner-left,
.ui-corner-tl {
  border-top-left-radius: 0;
}
```

The following screenshot shows how this changes the theme:

We can do this for each corner. Asymmetrical corner definitions are often used by web designers to good effect. In this case, we are going to change all the corner definitions but to the same value.

The theme says that each corner should have a radius of 4 pixels. Because each corner only covers a 90 degree segment of a circle and the center of the circle occupies 1 pixel of its own, it is considered good practice to set the corner radius value to an odd number for small values. Here, we are going to use a value of 3 pixels or 3px.

> The odd number is a rule of thumb. It helps keep things looking nice when pages are zoomed in.

We edit the preceding rule so that it looks like this:

```
.ui-corner-all,
.ui-corner-top,
.ui-corner-left,
.ui-corner-tl {
  border-top-left-radius: 3px;
}
```

Then, change the other three rules in exactly the same way.

 CSS allows us to have rules defined in separate parts. The entire rule is the sum of all the definitions applied in the order in which they are defined. Thus, `.ui-corner-all` actually has all the four corners defined.

Changing the shadow effects

In this section, we will examine the rules that define how shadow effects should look.

Shadow effects are pseudo-3D effects used by jQuery UI and PrimeFaces to great effect when overlays are used. An overlay is a component that is laid out above the rest of the page. They also cover up content in the background. To exaggerate the three-dimensional effect, a shadow effect is used.

An example of an overlay with a shadow effect can be seen in the following screenshot:

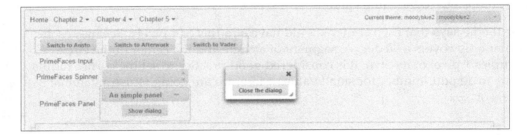

The dialog box in the middle is displayed as an overlay. The background is actually covered by a so-called curtain and it has a shadow that makes it stand out above the background even more.

The last two rules in our theme, `.ui-widget-overlay` and `.ui-widget-shadow`, define the curtain that covers the background content and the shadow attached to the dialog box.

The overlay rule looks like this:

```
.ui-widget-overlay {
  background: #aaaaaa url("#{resource['primefaces-
    moodyblue2:images/ui-bg_flat_0_aaaaaa_40x100.png']}") 50% 50%
    repeat-x;
```

```
    opacity: .3;
    filter: Alpha(Opacity=30);
}
```

The `background` definition is familiar to us now. The other definitions are new and define the opacity of the component that uses the rule. Here's a quote from w3schools.com (`http://www.w3schools.com/`):

> *The opacity property sets the opacity level for an element. The opacity-level describes the transparency-level, where 1 is not transparent at all, 0.5 is 50% see-through, and 0 is completely transparent.*

However, there are two properties defined — `opacity` and `filter`. These do actually define the same thing, but they define them for different browsers. The first property, opacity, works for all modern browsers, including version 9 or above of Internet Explorer. The second property, filter, is there to support the older versions of Internet Explorer. The `filter` sets the `Alpha` channel of the component background. The `Alpha` channel is the color channel that describes the transparency of a component. The other color channels are red, green, and blue in the RGB coordinate color system.

Although we are not going to change this rule, it is important that we examine it because it gives us a concrete example of how to set the opacity of components and account for browser differences in the process.

The second rule, `.ui-widget-shadow`, is an important one and it looks like this:

```
.ui-widget-shadow {
  margin: 2px 0 0 0;
  padding: 2px;
  background: #222255 url("#{resource['primefaces-
    moodyblue2:images/ui-bg_highlight-
    soft_30_222255_1x100.png']}") 50% top repeat-x;
  opacity: .3;
  filter: Alpha(Opacity=30);
  border-radius: 2px;
}
```

If you examine the dialog box displayed in the Mini Showcase page, you may discover something odd. PrimeFaces supplies its own shadow rule, `ui-shadow`. This means that this part of our theme might not actually be used. The `.ui-shadow` rule looks nothing like the `.ui-widget-shadow` rule. This is because PrimeFaces uses the new `box-shadow` property to define these. The results of the `.ui-widget-shadow` are not that visually pleasing. The only problem is that the older versions of Internet Explorer do not support this property, not that this really is a problem.

Here's a quote taken from w3schools.com (`http://www.w3schools.com/`):

> *The box-shadow property attaches one or more shadows to an element. The property is a comma-separated list of shadows, each specified by 2-4 length values, an optional color, and an optional inset keyword. Omitted lengths are 0.*

To explain this property, we will take the one defined by PrimeFaces and show it here:

```
.ui-shadow {
    -moz-box-shadow: 0px 5px 10px rgba(0,0,0,0.8);
    -webkit-box-shadow: 0px 5px 10px rgba(0,0,0,0.8);
    box-shadow: 0px 5px 10px rgba(0,0,0,0.8);
}
```

Now, we have three different properties, and all define the same thing. The `-moz-` and `-webkit-` prefixes are there for backend support for older versions of Firefox/ Mozilla (`-moz-`) and Chrome/Safari (`-webkit-`) before the CSS3 rules became finalized as a standard. Opera practiced supporting CSS3 from the beginning, and the more modern the version, the more the CSS3 properties are supported. The `box-shadow` property has been supported from the beginning.

The values are, in order:

1. **Horizontal shadow distance**: With positive values, this offsets the shadow to the right of the component. This value is required, and negative values are allowed.

2. **Vertical shadow distance**: With positive values, this offsets the shadow below the bottom of the component. This value is required, and negative values are allowed.

3. **Blur**: This sets the size of the blurred region for the shadow. This value is optional, and negative values make no sense.

4. **Spread**: This sets the size of the shadow. This value is optional, and negative values result in a shadow being cast which is smaller than the component being shadowed.

5. **Color**: This sets the color of the shadow. The default value is black. By using a color defined by using the `rgba` function, you can set the opacity of the shadow.

So, the defined `box-shadow` property is set horizontally central to the component and is 5 pixels lower than the component. The blurred region occupies 10 pixels. The color is black with an `opacity` property of 80%.

Apart from the aesthetic advantage of using `box-shadow`, a shadow can also be rendered using the outline of the component that it is shadowing. This means that we do not need to worry about the corner radii for instance.

We are going to add our own definition of `.ui-shadow` and change the color of the shadow to a dark blue, as follows:

```
.ui-shadow {
  -moz-box-shadow: 0px 5px 10px rgba(0,0,64,0.8);
  -webkit-box-shadow: 0px 5px 10px rgba(0,0,64,0.8);
  box-shadow: 0px 5px 10px rgba(0,0,64,0.8);
}
```

Now, when you check the dialog box shadow, you will discover that nothing has changed! This is the case because we are attempting to redefine a rule, which is okay, but the order in which the CSS is applied is also important. Rules applied later take precedence over earlier rules. If you check the network activity when you reload the page, you will see the following:

The `theme.css` file is being loaded before the PrimeFaces component's CSS file. So, the rules that we define and which attempt to redefine the rules in the PrimeFaces component's CSS will not work because of the way the rule precedence for CSS works. We fix this simply by using the `!important` notation, which ensures that the `!important` rules have precedence over rules that are not defined as being `!important` regardless of the order in which they are defined.

The rule now looks like this:

```
.ui-shadow {
  -moz-box-shadow: 0px 5px 10px rgba(0,0,64,0.8) !important;
  -webkit-box-shadow: 0px 5px 10px rgba(0,0,64,0.8) !important;
  box-shadow: 0px 5px 10px rgba(0,0,64,0.8) !important;
}
```

We now have a dark blue shadow, as shown in the following screenshot:

Note that now, any component that either is or has a pop-up element also has a shadow. This means that our menu and the ThemeSwitcher also have the same shadow.

In this section, we learned how PrimeFaces has its own, better, CSS rule to create shadows and how PrimeFaces loads the CSS resources. We also learned how to change the PrimeFaces `.ui-shadow` rule and how to ensure that our rule has precedence over the PrimeFaces component's rule.

Changing the menu background

In the last section of this chapter, we are going to change the menu bar, menu, and menu list backgrounds to the same background as that of the other components.

As mentioned earlier in this chapter, the menu bar, menu, and menu list components are rather bland. This is because we used ThemeRoller to create the basis for our theme, and this doesn't have anything to do with a component-specific look and feel. At most, the content of the menu bar, menu, and menu lists will be defined as widget content. If we only want to change the way the menu bar, menu, and menu list content looks, we have to be more specific when changing or creating rules. If you examine the HTML for the menu bar, you will see the rules that are defined for its look and feel:

```
class="ui-menu ui-menubar ui-widget ui-widget-content ui-corner-
all ui-helper-clearfix"
```

Apart from the `ui-helper-clearfix` rule, which simply sets browsers' default values to common values, we have the usual `ui-widget ui-widget-content` and `ui-corner-all` rules, which you should now be familiar with.

The `ui-menu` and `ui-menubar` rules are not part of the CSS theme and therefore, they must be component-specific. Does this mean that we can add properties to these rules in order to achieve the desired affect?

Add the following to `theme.css`, close to our rule for `label`:

```
/* Menu, menu bar */
.ui-menu, .ui-menubar {
  background: #ccccff url("#{resource['primefaces-
    moodyblue2:images/ui-bg_highlight-
    soft_75_ccccff_1x100.png']}") 50% 50% repeat-x;
}
```

The following screenshot shows how things now look:

As you can see, the menus and menu bar now look as we want them to, but the menu list is still bland. Therefore, we need to add at least one more rule to make things work. To find out which rule or rules we need to change, we need to examine the menu list to see which rules are used for them.

For each individual menu item in the list, we can use the `ui-menuitem` rule. If we define this, then each menu item will have the same background as the rest of our components. So, we add the following to the rule that we created in `theme.css`:

```
/* Menu, menu bar */
.ui-menu, .ui-menubar, .ui-menuitem {
  background: #ccccff url("#{resource['primefaces-
    moodyblue2:images/ui-bg_highlight-
    soft_75_ccccff_1x100.png']}") 50% 50% repeat-x;
}
```

The following screenshot shows that things are still not quite how we want them to look:

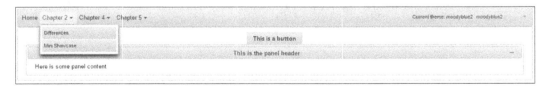

There is a white border around each menu item. Worse still, the selected menu items look terrible. My screenshot tool was unable to capture how bad it looked and we aren't interested in terrible anyway.

If we cannot adequately set the look and feel for each individual menu item, what about the list itself?

 This has already been done in the **Aristo** theme, but we used background gradient colors.

Each menu item is actually **a list component** in an unordered list. So, the parent of the menu items, which is the menu list, must be an HTML `ul` component. The immediate parent `ul` component has a class of `ui-menu-list` and `ui-menu-child`.

If you examine the differences between the two rules, you will see that `.ui-menu-list` simply sets the border to none. The `.ui-menu-child` rule sets the width to 100%. We want our changes to be strongly associated with a layout of 100%. Therefore, we change our rule to redefine `.ui-menu-child` instead of `.ui-menuitem`.

We still have a problem. The background doesn't cover the entire menu list vertically.

We need to associate the rule that we define with the parent of the menu child to ensure that a menu child contained by a menu parent is referred to. We also don't need to create a rule for `ui-menubar` either. Lastly, we need to ensure that the background image fills completely. So, we will remove the starting positions.

The final rule looks like this:

```
/* Menu, menu children */
.ui-menu, .ui-menu-parent .ui-menu-child {
  background: #ccccff url("#{resource['primefaces-
    moodyblue2:images/ui-bg_highlight-
    soft_75_ccccff_1x100.png']}") repeat-x;
}
```

Summary

In this chapter, we explored the structure of a theme and the rules that we need to change in order to tweak our theme to make it even better. We also learned how to override the PrimeFaces component rules and make sure that our rules have precedence over them. We saw that PrimeFaces also uses more modern CSS rules than the ones that jQuery UI uses where appropriate and that we can change these rules as well. We also became comfortable defining new rules by associating our theme with specific component types. It was demonstrated that although a PrimeFaces theme is about how things look like on a page, we are not restricted to the general rules provided by ThemeRoller to achieve our aims.

In the next chapter, we are going to discover how PrimeFaces uses icon sprites, how we can provide our own icons, how to add new icons that are not already provided, and how to use Font Awesome icons in PrimeFaces application.

6
Icons

Icons add a lot of value to an application based on the principle that a picture is worth a thousand words. Equally important is the fact that they can, when well designed, please the eye and serve as memory joggers for your user. We humans strongly associate symbols with actions. For example, a `save` button with a *disc* icon is more evocative. The association becomes even stronger when we use the same icon for the same action in menus and button bars. It is also possible to use icons in place of text labels. It is an important thing to keep in mind when designing the user interface of your application that the navigational and action elements (such as buttons) should not be so intrusive that the application becomes too cluttered with the things that can be done. The user wants to be able to see the information that they want to see and use input dialogs to add more. What they don't want is to be distracted with links, lots of link and button text, and glaring visuals.

In this chapter, we will cover the following topics:

- The standard theme icon set
- Creating a set of icons of our own
- Adding new icons to a theme
- Using custom icons in a `commandButton` component
- Using custom icons in a `menu` component
- The Font Awesome icons as an alternative to the ThemeRoller icons

Introducing the standard theme icon set

jQuery UI provides a big set of standard icons that can be applied by just adding icon class names to HTML elements. The full list of icons is available at its official site, which can be viewed by visiting `http://api.jqueryui.com/theming/icons/`.

Also, available in some of the published icon cheat sheets at http://www.petefreitag.com/cheatsheets/jqueryui-icons/.

The icon class names follow the following syntax in order to add them for HTML elements:

.ui-icon-{icon type}-{icon sub description}-{direction}

For example, the following span element will display an icon of a triangle pointing to the south:

```
<span class="ui-icon ui-icon-triangle-1-s"></span>
```

Other icons such as ui-icon-triangle-1-n, ui-icon-triangle-1-e, and ui-icon-triangle-1-w represent icons of triangles pointing to the north, east, and west respectively. The direction element is optional, and it is available only for a few icons such as a triangle, an arrow, and so on.

These theme icons will be integrated in a number of jQuery UI-based widgets such as buttons, menus, dialogs, date picker components, and so on.

The aforementioned standard set of icons is available in the ThemeRoller as one **image sprite** instead of a separate image for each icon. That is, ThemeRoller is designed to use the image sprites technology for icons. The different image sprites that vary in color (based on the widget state) are available in the images folder of each downloaded theme.

An image sprite is a collection of images put into a single image. A webpage with many images may take a long time to load and generate multiple server requests. For a high-performance application, this idea will reduce the number of server requests and bandwidth. Also, it centralizes the image locations so that all the icons can be found at one location.

The basic image sprite for the PrimeFaces Aristo theme looks like this:

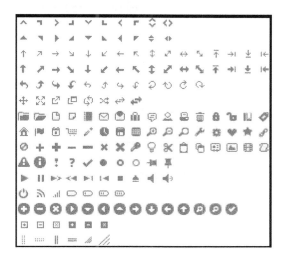

The image sprite's look and feel will vary based on the screen area of the widget and its components such as the header and content and widget states such as hover, active, highlight, and error styles.

Let us now consider a JSF/PF-based example, where we can add a standard set of icons for UI components such as the commandButton and menu bar.

First, we will create a new folder in web pages called chapter6. Then, we will create a new JSF template client called standardThemeIcons.xhtml and add a link to it in the chaptersTemplate.xhtml template file. When adding a submenu, use Chapter 6 for the label name and for the menu item, use Standard Icon Set as its value.

In the title section, replace the text title with the respective topic of this chapter, which is Standard Icons:

```
<ui:define name="title">
   Standard Icons
</ui:define>
```

In the content section, replace the text content with the code for commandButton and menu components.

Let's start with the `commandButton` components. The set of `commandButton` components uses the standard theme icon set with the help of the `icon` attribute, as follows:

```
<h:panelGroup style="margin-left:830px">
  <h3 style="margin-top: 0">Buttons</h3>
  <p:commandButton value="Edit" icon="ui-icon-pencil"
  type="button" />
  <p:commandButton value="Bookmark" icon="ui-icon-bookmark"
  type="button" />
  <p:commandButton value="Next" icon="ui-icon-circle-arrow-e"
  type="button" />
  <p:commandButton value="Previous"
  icon="ui-icon-circle-arrow-w" type="button" />
</h:panelGroup>
```

The generated HTML for the first `commandButton` that is used to display the standard icon will be as follows:

```
<button id="mainForm:j_idt15" name="mainForm:j_idt15"
class="ui-button ui-widget ui-state-default ui-corner-all
ui-button-text-icon-left" type="button" role="button"
aria-disabled="false">
  <span class="ui-button-icon-left ui-icon ui-c
  ui-icon-pencil"></span>
  <span class="ui-button-text ui-c">Edit</span>
</button>
```

The PrimeFaces `commandButton` renderer appends the icon position CSS class based on the icon position (left or right) to the HTML button element, apart from the icon CSS class in one child span element and text CSS class in another child span element. This way, it displays the icon on `commandButton` based on the icon position property. By default, the position of the icon is `left`.

Now, we will move on to the `menu` components. A `menu` component uses the standard theme icon set with the help of the `menu` item icon attribute. Add the following code snippets of the `menu` component to your page:

```
<h3>Menu</h3>
<p:menu style="margin-left:500px">
  <p:submenu label="File">
    <p:menuitem value="New" url="#" icon="ui-icon-plus" />
    <p:menuitem value="Delete" url="#" icon="ui-icon-close" />
    <p:menuitem value="Refresh" url="#"
      icon="ui-icon-refresh" />
```

```
    <p:menuitem value="Print" url="#" icon="ui-icon-print" />
  </p:submenu>
  <p:submenu label="Navigations">
    <p:menuitem value="Home" url="http://www.primefaces.org"
      icon="ui-icon home" />
    <p:menuitem value="Admin" url="#" icon="ui-icon-person" />
    <p:menuitem value="Contact Us" url="#"
    icon="ui-icon-contact" />
  </p:submenu>
</p:menu>
```

You may have observed from the preceding code snippets that each icon from ThemeRoller starts with ui-icon for consistency.

Now, run the application and navigate your way to the newly created page, and you should see the standard ThemeRoller icons applied to buttons and menu items, as shown in the following screenshot:

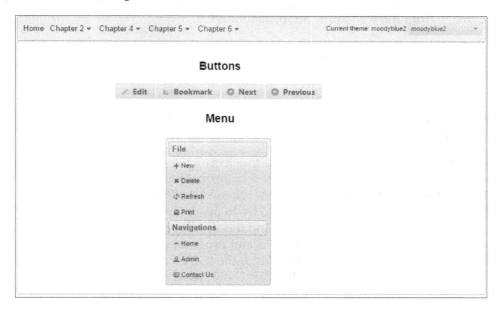

For further information, you can use PrimeFaces showcase (http://www. primefaces.org/showcase/), where you can see the default icons used for components, applying standard theme icons with the help of the icon attribute, and so on.

Creating a set of icons of our own

In this section, we are going to discuss how to create our own icons for the PrimeFaces web application. Instead of using images, you need to use image sprites by considering the impact of application performance.

Most of the time, we might be interested in adding custom icons to UI components apart from the regular standard icon set. Generally, in order to create our own custom icons, we need to provide CSS classes with the `background-image` property, which is referred to the image in the theme `images` folder.

For example, the following `commandButton` components will use a custom icon:

```
<p:commandButton value="With Icon" icon="disk"/>
<p:commandButton icon="disk"/>
```

The `disk` icon is created by adding the `.disk` CSS class with the background image property. In order to display the image, you need to provide the correct relative path of the image from the web application, as follows:

```
.disk {
    background-image: url('disk.png') !important;

}
```

However, as discussed earlier, we are going to use the image sprite technology instead of a separate image for each icon to optimize web performance.

Before creating an image sprite, you need to select all the required images and convert those images (PNG, JPG, and so on) to the icon format with a size almost equal to to that of the ThemeRoller icons. In this book, we used the **Paint.NET** tool to convert images to the ICO format with a size of 16 by 16 pixels. Paint.NET is a free raster graphics editor for Microsoft Windows, and it is developed on the .NET framework. It is a good replacement for the Microsoft Paint program in an editor with support for layers blending, transparency, and plugins. If the ICO format is not available, then you have to add the file type plug-in for the Paint.NET installation directory.

So, this is just a two-step process for the conversion:

1. The image (PNG, JPG, and so on) need to be saved as the Icons (`*.ico`) option from the **Save as type** dropdown.
2. Then, select 16 by 16 dimensions with the supported bit system (8-bit, 32-bit, and so on). All the PrimeFaces theme icons are designed to have the same dimensions.

There are many online and offline tools available that can be used to create an image sprite. I used Instant Sprite, an open source CSS sprite generator tool, to create an image sprite in this chapter. You can have a look at the official site for this CSS generator tool by visiting `http://instantsprite.com/`.

Let's go through the following step-by-step process to create an image sprite using the Instant Sprite tool:

1. First, either select multiple icons from your computer, or drag and drop icons on to the tool page.

2. In the **Thumbnails** section, just drag and drop the images to change their order in the sprite.

3. Change the offset (in pixels), direction (horizontal, vertical, and diagonal), and the type (`.png` or `.gif`) values in the **Options** section.

4. In the **Sprite** section, right-click on the image to save it on your computer. You can also save the image in a new window or as a base64 type.

5. In the **Usage** section, you will find the generated sprite CSS classes and HTML.

6. Once the image is created, you will be able to see the image in the preview section before finalizing the image.

Now, let's start creating the image sprite for `button` bar and `menu` components, which are going to be used in later sections.

First, download or copy the required individual icons on the computer. Then, select all those files and drag and drop them in a particular order, as follows:

```
┌─ Thumbnails ──────────────────────────────────────────────────────┐
│                                                                    │
│  You can drag and drop the images to change their order in the sprite. │
│                                                                    │
│   ✖  │ 📝 edit.ico              [ type: image/x-icon | size: 1.12 kb ] │
│   ✖  │ 🔖 bookmark.ico          [ type: image/x-icon | size: 1.12 kb ] │
│   ✖  │ 🔄 next.ico              [ type: image/x-icon | size: 1.12 kb ] │
│   ✖  │ 🔄 previous.ico          [ type: image/x-icon | size: 1.12 kb ] │
│   ✖  │ 📄 new.ico               [ type: image/x-icon | size: 1.12 kb ] │
│   ✖  │ ❎ delete.ico            [ type: image/x-icon | size: 1.12 kb ] │
│   ✖  │ 🔄 refresh.ico           [ type: image/x-icon | size: 1.12 kb ] │
│   ✖  │ 🖨 print.ico             [ type: image/x-icon | size: 1.12 kb ] │
│   ✖  │ 🏠 home.ico              [ type: image/x-icon | size: 1.12 kb ] │
│   ✖  │ 👤 admin.ico             [ type: image/x-icon | size: 1.12 kb ] │
│   ✖  │ 💬 contactus.ico         [ type: image/x-icon | size: 1.12 kb ] │
│                                                                    │
└────────────────────────────────────────────────────────────────────┘
```

We can also configure a few options, such as an offset of 10 px for icon padding, direction as horizontal to display them horizontally, and then finally selecting the image as the PNG type:

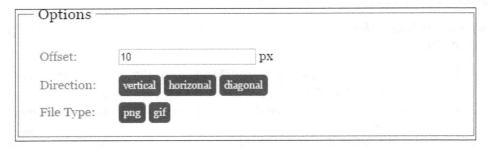

The image sprite is generated in the sprite section, as follows:

Right-click on the image to save it on your computer. Now, we have created a custom image sprite from the set of icons. Once the image sprite has been created, change the sprite name to `ui-custom-icons` and copy the generated CSS styles for later.

```
┌─ Usage ──────────────────────────────────────────────────────────────────
  You can use a RegExp object for capturing the file name.

  CSS prefix   ui-icon  .class prefix  (.*)  class suffix   { ... }
  ┌──────────────────────────────────────────────────────────────────────┐
  │ .ui-icon { background: url('ui-icon.png') no-repeat top left; width: 16px; height: 16px;  } │
  │ .ui-icon.edit { background-position: 0 0; }                            │
  │ .ui-icon.bookmark { background-position: -26px 0; }                    │
  │ .ui-icon.next { background-position: -52px 0; }                        │
  │ .ui-icon.previous { background-position: -78px 0; }                    │
  │ .ui-icon.new { background-position: -104px 0; }                        │
  │ .ui-icon.delete { background-position: -130px 0; }                     │
  │ .ui-icon.refresh { background-position: -156px 0; }                    │
  │ .ui-icon.print { background-position: -182px 0; }                      │
  │ .ui-icon.home { background-position: -208px 0; }                       │
  │ .ui-icon.admin { background-position: -234px 0; }                      │
  │ .ui-icon.contactus { background-position: -260px 0; }                  │
  └──────────────────────────────────────────────────────────────────────┘
  ┌──────────────────────────────────────────────────────────────────────┐
  │ <div class='ui-icon edit'></div>                                       │
  │ <div class='ui-icon bookmark'></div>                                   │
  │ <div class='ui-icon next'></div>                                       │
  │ <div class='ui-icon previous'></div>                                   │
  │ <div class='ui-icon new'></div>                                        │
  │ <div class='ui-icon delete'></div>                                     │
  │ <div class='ui-icon refresh'></div>                                    │
  │ <div class='ui-icon print'></div>                                      │
  │ <div class='ui-icon home'></div>                                       │
  │ <div class='ui-icon admin'></div>                                      │
  │ <div class='ui-icon contactus'></div>                                  │
  └──────────────────────────────────────────────────────────────────────┘
```

In the generated HTML, note that each `div` class is appended with the `ui-icon` class to display the icon with a width of 16 px and height of 16 px.

Adding the new icons to your theme

In order to apply the custom icons to your web page, we first need to copy the generated image sprite file and then add the generated CSS classes from the previous section.

The following generated sprite file has to be added to the `images` folder of the `primefaces-moodyBlue2` custom theme. Let's name the file `ui-custom-icons`:

After this, copy the generated CSS rules from the previous section.

The first CSS class (`ui-icon`) contains the image sprite to display custom icons using the background URL property and dimensions such as the `width` and `height` properties for each icon. But since we are going to add the image reference in widget state style classes, you need to remove the background image URL property from the `ui-icon` class. Hence, the `ui-icon` class contains only the `width` and `height` dimensions:

```
.ui-icon {
  width: 16px;
  height: 16px;
}
```

Later, modify the icon-specific CSS class names as shown in the following format. Each icon has its own icon name:

```
.ui-icon-{icon name}
```

The following CSS classes are used to refer individual icons with the help of the `background-position` property. Now after modification, the positioning CSS classes will look like this:

```
.ui-icon-edit { background-position: 0 0; }
.ui-icon-bookmark { background-position: -26px 0; }
.ui-icon-next { background-position: -52px 0; }
```

```
.ui-icon-previous { background-position: -78px 0; }
.ui-icon-new { background-position: -104px 0; }
.ui-icon-delete { background-position: -130px 0; }
.ui-icon-refresh { background-position: -156px 0; }
.ui-icon-print { background-position: -182px 0; }
.ui-icon-home { background-position: -208px 0; }
.ui-icon-admin { background-position: -234px 0; }
.ui-icon-contactus { background-position: -260px 0; }
```

Apart from the preceding CSS classes, we have to add the component state CSS classes. Widget states such as hover, focus, highlight, active, and error need to refer to different image sprites in order to display the component state behavior for user interactions. For demonstration purposes, we created only one image sprite and used it for all the CSS classes. But in real-time development, the image will vary based on the widget state.

The following widget states refer to image sprites for different widget states:

```
.ui-icon,
.ui-widget-content .ui-icon {
  background-image: url("#{resource['primefaces-
  moodyblue2:images/ui-custom-icons.png']}");
}
.ui-widget-header .ui-icon {
  background-image: url("#{resource['primefaces-
  moodyblue2:images/ui-custom-icons.png']}");
}
.ui-state-default .ui-icon {
  background-image: url("#{resource['primefaces-
  moodyblue2:images/ui-custom-icons.png']}");
}
.ui-state-hover .ui-icon,
.ui-state-focus .ui-icon {
  background-image: url("#{resource['primefaces-
  moodyblue2:images/ui-custom-icons.png']}");
}
.ui-state-active .ui-icon {
  background-image: url("#{resource['primefaces-
  moodyblue2:images/ui-custom-icons.png']}");
}
.ui-state-highlight .ui-icon {
  background-image: url("#{resource['primefaces-
  moodyblue2:images/ui-custom-icons.png']}");
}
.ui-state-error .ui-icon,
.ui-state-error-text .ui-icon {
  background-image: url("#{resource['primefaces-
  moodyblue2:images/ui-custom-icons.png']}");
}
```

In the JSF ecosystem, image references in the `theme.css` file must be converted to an expression that JSF resource loading can understand.

So at first, in the preceding CSS classes, all the image URLs are appeared in the following expression:

```
background-image: url("images/ui-custom-icons.png");
```

The preceding expression, when modified, looks like this:

```
background-image: url("#{resource['primefaces-
moodyblue2:images/ui-custom-icons.png']}");
```

We need to make sure that the default state classes are commented out in the `theme.css` (the `moodyblue2` theme) file to display the custom icons. By default, custom theme classes (such as the state classes and icon classes available under custom states and images and custom icons positioning) are commented out in the source code of the GitHub project. So, we need to uncomment these sections and comment out the default theme classes (such as the state classes and icon classes available under states and images and positioning). This means that the default or custom style classes only need to be available in the `theme.css` file.

(OR)

You can see all these changes in **moodyblue3** theme as well. The **custom icons** appeared in Custom Icons screen by just changing the current theme to `moodyblue3`.

Using custom icons in the commandButton components

After applying the new icons to the theme, you are ready to use them on the PrimeFaces components. In this section, we will add custom icons to command buttons. Let's add a link named `Custom Icons` to the `chaptersTemplate.xhtml` file. The title of this page is also named `Custom Icons`.

The following code snippets show how custom icons are added to command buttons using the icon attribute:

```
<h3 style="margin-top: 0">Buttons</h3>
<p:commandButton value="Edit" icon="ui-icon-edit" type="button" />
```

```
<p:commandButton value="Bookmark" icon="ui-icon-bookmark"
type="button" />
<p:commandButton value="Next" icon="ui-icon-next" type="button" />
<p:commandButton value="Previous" icon="ui-icon-previous"
type="button" />
```

Now, run the application and navigate to the newly created page. You should see the custom icons applied to the command buttons, as shown in the following screenshot:

The `commandButton` component also supports the `iconpos` attribute if you wish to display the icon either to the left or right side. The default value is `left`.

Using custom icons in a menu component

In this section, we are going to add custom icons to a `menu` component. The `menuitem` tag supports the `icon` attribute to attach a custom icon.

The following code snippets show how custom icons are added to the `menu` component:

```
<h3>Menu</h3>
<p:menu style="margin-left:500px">
  <p:submenu label="File">
    <p:menuitem value="New" url="#" icon="ui-icon-new" />
    <p:menuitem value="Delete" url="#" icon="ui-icon-delete" />
    <p:menuitem value="Refresh" url="#" icon="ui-icon-refresh" />
    <p:menuitem value="Print" url="#" icon="ui-icon-print" />
  </p:submenu>
  <p:submenu label="Navigations">
    <p:menuitem value="Home" url="http://www.primefaces.org"
    icon="ui-icon-home" />
    <p:menuitem value="Admin" url="#" icon="ui-icon-admin" />
    <p:menuitem value="Contact Us" url="#"
    icon="ui-icon-contactus" />
  </p:submenu>
</p:menu>
```

Now, run the application and navigate to the newly created page. You will see the custom icons applied to the menu component, as shown in the following screenshot:

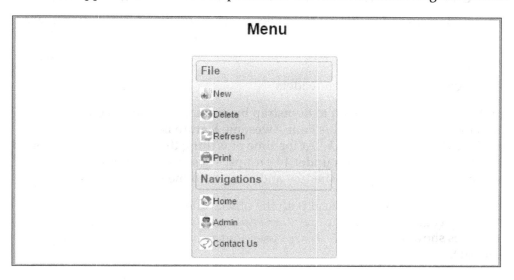

Thus, you can apply custom icons on a PrimeFaces component that supports the icon attribute.

The Font Awesome icons as an alternative to the ThemeRoller icons

In addition to the default ThemeRoller icon set, the PrimeFaces team provided and supported a set of alternative icons named the **Font Awesome** iconic font and CSS framework. Originally, it was designed for the **Twitter Bootstrap** frontend framework. Currently, it works well with all frameworks. The official site for the Font Awesome toolkit is http://fortawesome.github.io/Font-Awesome/.

The features of Font Awesome that make it a powerful iconic font and CSS toolkit are as follows:

- **One font, 519 icons**: In a single collection, Font Awesome is a pictographic language of web-related actions
- **No JavaScript required**: It has minimum compatibility issues because Font Awesome doesn't required JavaScript
- **Infinite scalability**: SVG (short for **Scalable Vector Graphics**) icons look awesome in any size

- **Free to use**: It is completely free and can be used for commercial usage
- **CSS control**: It's easy to style the icon color, size, shadow, and so on
- **Perfect on retina displays**: It looks gorgeous on high resolution displays
- It can be easily integrated with all frameworks
- Desktop-friendly
- Compatible with screen readers

Font Awesome is an extension to Bootstrap by providing various icons based on scalable vector graphics. This Font Awesome feature is available from the PrimeFaces 5.2 release onwards. At the time of writing this book, there are around 519 highly customizable icons under 14 groups. These icons can be customized in terms of size, color, drop and shadow and so on with the power of CSS.

The full list of icons is available at both the official site of Font Awesome (http://fortawesome.github.io/Font-Awesome/icons/) as well as the PrimeFaces showcase (http://www.primefaces.org/showcase/ui/misc/fa.xhtml).

In order to enable this feature, we have to set primefaces.FONT_AWESOME context param in web.xml to true, as follows:

```
<context-param>
  <param-name>primefaces.FONT_AWESOME</param-name>
  <param-value>true</param-value>
</context-param>
```

The usage is as simple as using the standard ThemeRoller icons. PrimeFaces components such as buttons or menu items provide an icon attribute, which accepts an icon from the Font Awesome icon set. Remember that the icons should be prefixed by fa in a component.

The general syntax of the Font Awesome icons will be as follows:

```
fa fa-[name]-[shape]-[o]-[direction]
```

Here, [name] is the name of the icon, [shape] is the optional shape of the icon's background (either circle or square), [o] is the optional outlined version of the icon, and [direction] is the direction in which certain icons point.

Now, we first create a new navigation link named `FontAwesome` under `chapter6` inside the `chapterTemplate.xhtml` template file. Then, we create a JSF template client called `fontawesome.xhtml`, where it explains the Font Awesome feature with the help of buttons and menu. This page has been added as a menu item for the top-level menu bar.

In the content section, replace the text content with the following code snippets.

The following set of buttons displays the Font Awesome icons with the help of the icon attribute. You may have observed that the `fa-fw` style class used to set icons at a fixed width. This is useful when variable widths throw off alignment:

```
<h3 style="margin-top: 0">Buttons</h3>
<p:commandButton value="Edit" icon="fa fa-fw fa-edit"
  type="button" />
<p:commandButton value="Bookmark" icon="fa fa-fw fa-bookmark"
  type="button" />
<p:commandButton value="Next" icon="fa fa-fw fa-arrow-right"
  type="button" />
<p:commandButton value="Previous" icon="fa fa-fw fa-arrow-
  left" type="button" />
```

After this, apply the Font Awesome icons to navigation lists, such as the menu component, to display the icons just to the left of the component text content, as follows:

```
<h3>Menu</h3>
<p:menu style="margin-left:500px">
  <p:submenu label="File">
    <p:menuitem value="New" url="#" icon="fa fa-plus" />
    <p:menuitem value="Delete" url="#" icon="fa fa-close" />
    <p:menuitem value="Refresh" url="#" icon="fa fa-refresh" />
    <p:menuitem value="Print" url="#" icon="fa fa-print" />
  </p:submenu>
  <p:submenu label="Navigations">
    <p:menuitem value="Home" url="http://www.primefaces.org"
    icon="fa fa-home" />
    <p:menuitem value="Admin" url="#" icon="fa fa-user" />
    <p:menuitem value="Contact Us" url="#"
    icon="fa fa-picture-o" />
  </p:submenu>
</p:menu>
```

Now, run the application and navigate to the newly created page. You should see the Font Awesome icons applied to buttons and menu items, as shown in the following screenshot:

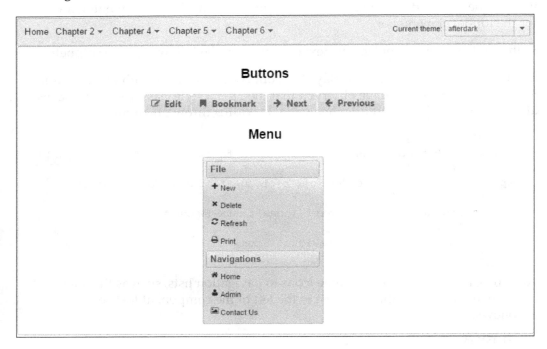

 Note that the 40 shiny new icons of Font Awesome are available only in the PrimeFaces Elite 5.2.2 release and the community PrimeFaces 5.3 release because PrimeFaces was upgraded to Font Awesome 4.3 version since its 5.2.2 release.

Summary

In this chapter, we explored the standard theme icon set and how to use it on various PrimeFaces components. We also learned how to create our own set of icons in the form of the image sprite technology. We saw how to create image sprites using open source online tools and add them on a PrimeFaces theme. Finally, we had a look at the Font Awesome CSS framework, which was introduced as an alternative to the standard ThemeRoller icons. To ensure best practice, we learned how to use icons on `commandButton` and `menu` components. Now that you've come to the end of this chapter, you should be comfortable using web icons for PrimeFaces components in different ways.

In the next chapter, we are going to discover how to enhance the PrimeFaces components' state based on the underlying data, use a combination of JavaScript and CSS for dynamic changes, and use the PrimeFaces utility methods for dynamic changes without using any JavaScript.

7
Dynamic Changes – a Working Example

In this chapter, we will explore how to use a combination of JavaScript and CSS to enhance an application. Themes can only do so much and, quite often, we want to enhance the way a PrimeFaces component looks depending on the state of the underlying data.

The following is a list of the topics that will be covered in this chapter:

* Introducing the Schedule component
* The problem with the currently selected date and event
* Creating a CSS rule to set a background color in an HTML element
* Creating a JavaScript function to apply that CSS rule to a specific HTML element
* Executing a client-side JavaScript function from the server-side – the power of AJAX and the `RequestContext` utility

Introducing the schedule component

In the previous chapters of this book, we have learned how to enhance a PrimeFaces component's look and feel in different ways, with the help of a theme, such as overriding the standard CSS rules, applying various built-in PrimeFaces themes, creating custom themes using ThemeRoller, adding built-in and custom icons, and so on.

We can also extend a PrimeFaces component's look and feel, depending on the state of the underlying data, by performing dynamic changes using web technologies such as JavaScript, CSS, AJAX, and the `RequestContext` utilities from PrimeFaces API. We'll demonstrate these dynamic changes with the help of the multifeatured schedule component.

Schedule provides an Outlook calendar; an **iCal**-like JSF component to manage events. It is a highly customizable widget featuring various views (month, week, day), a built-in **i18n** (internationalization), drag and drop, resize, a customizable event dialog box and AJAX listeners for user interactions, and so on.

Let us now take a JSF/PrimeFaces-based example, where we can see the schedule component with the default skinning behavior.

First we will create a new folder inside webapp folder inside `webapp` folder called `chapter7`. Then we will create a new JSF template client called `scheduleComponent.xhtml` and add a link to it in the `chaptersTemplate.xhtml` template file. When adding a submenu, use `Chapter 7` as the label and, for the menu item, use the `Schedule component` as its value.

In the `title` section, replace the text title with the respective topic of this chapter, which is `Schedule Component`:

```
<ui:define name="title">
  Schedule Component
</ui:define>
```

In the content section, replace the text content with the schedule component backing the code for schedule event model, as follows:

```
<p:schedule id="schedule"
  value="#{myScheduleView.scheduleEventModel}"
  widgetVar="myschedule" timeZone="GMT+2">
  <p:ajax event="dateSelect"
    listener="#{myScheduleView.onDateSelect}"
    update="eventDetails" oncomplete="PF('eventDialog').show();"/>
  <p:ajax event="eventSelect"
    listener="#{myScheduleView.onEventSelect}"
    update="eventDetails" oncomplete="PF('eventDialog').show();"/>
</p:schedule>
```

We also attach the `dateSelect` and `eventSelect` AJAX listeners to create the new event by selecting a particular date and working on the existing event by modifying its details. Each schedule event contains the `title`, `startDate`, `endDate`, and `allDay` properties needed to display event data on completion of date selection or event selection user interactions. The `dialog` component is used to display the event properties from the AJAX events, as follows:

```
<p:dialog widgetVar="eventDialog" header="Event Details"
  showEffect="clip" hideEffect="clip">
  <h:panelGrid id="eventDetails" columns="2">
    <h:outputLabel for="title" value="Title:" />
    <p:inputText id="title" value="#{myScheduleView.event.title}"
      required="true" />

    <h:outputLabel for="from" value="From:" />
    <p:inputMask id="from" value="#{myScheduleView.event.startDate}"
      mask="99/99/9999">
      <f:convertDateTime pattern="dd/MM/yyyy" timeZone="GMT+2"/>
    </p:inputMask>

    <h:outputLabel for="to" value="To:" />
    <p:inputMask id="to" value="#{myScheduleView.event.endDate}"
      mask="99/99/9999">
      <f:convertDateTime pattern="dd/MM/yyyy" timeZone="GMT+2"/>
    </p:inputMask>

    <h:outputLabel for="allDay" value="All Day:" />
    <h:selectBooleanCheckbox id="allDay"
      value="#{myScheduleView.event.allDay}" />

    <p:commandButton type="reset" value="Reset" />
    <p:commandButton id="addButton" value="Save"
      actionListener="#{myScheduleView.addEvent}"
      oncomplete="PF('myschedule').update();
      PF('eventDialog').hide();" />
  </h:panelGrid>
</p:dialog>
```

When you click on the **Save** button, the event details will be either created or updated from the given user input. If you apply PrimeFaces **PPR** (short for **partial page rendering**) to update the schedule component, then you may observe a UI lag, as the **Document Object Model (DOM)** will be generated and replaced. Fortunately, the schedule component provides a simple client-side API, which includes the `update()` method to save the bandwidth and increase the page load performance.

Before running the application, the backing event schedule model needs to be created by adding the events that occurred in the current month. This schedule model needs to be created inside the session-scoped MyScheduleView.java Bean, as follows:

```
private ScheduleModel scheduleEventModel;
private ScheduleEvent event = new DefaultScheduleEvent();
@PostConstruct
public void init() {
  scheduleEventModel = new DefaultScheduleModel();
  scheduleEventModel.addEvent(new DefaultScheduleEvent("Birthday
    Celebrations",today6Pm(), today11Pm()));
  scheduleEventModel.addEvent(new DefaultScheduleEvent(
    "Lunch at Hotel Grand", nextDay1Pm(), nextDay3Pm()));
  scheduleEventModel.addEvent(new DefaultScheduleEvent(
    "Shopping at City express", previousDay8Pm(),
    previousDay11Pm()));
  scheduleEventModel.addEvent(new DefaultScheduleEvent(
    "Tours and Trips all over the Europe",
    theDayAfter3Pm(),fourDaysLater3pm()));

}

public void addEvent(ActionEvent actionEvent) {
  if (event.getId() == null)
  scheduleEventModel.addEvent(event);
    else
  scheduleEventModel.updateEvent(event);

  event = new DefaultScheduleEvent();
}

//getters and setters
```

The first event from above ScheduleModel is created with *from date* and *to date* using below methods:

```
private Date today6Pm() {
  Calendar t = (Calendar) today().clone();
  t.set(Calendar.AM_PM, Calendar.PM);
  t.set(Calendar.HOUR, 6);
  return t.getTime();
}
```

```
private Date today11Pm() {
  Calendar t = (Calendar) today().clone();
  t.set(Calendar.AM_PM, Calendar.PM);
  t.set(Calendar.HOUR, 11);
  return t.getTime();
}
// Add remaining date (from date and to date) methods for each event
```

 For more details, the full code is available in the chapter07 folder of the GitHub PFThemes project.

Now run the application and navigate to the newly created page. You will see the schedule component with the existing events, as shown in the following screenshot:

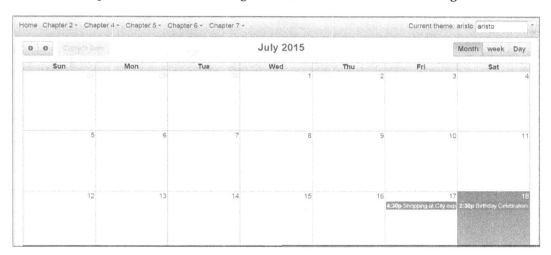

You may have also noted that the schedule view can be changed to the month, week, and day views. Apart from the regular features of the schedule component, you can also add lazy loading, a customized header, an event limit, and local support, but these features are beyond the scope and goals of this book.

A lack of skinning support for date and event selection

Let us now try to attach AJAX listener methods for date and event selection to display event properties in a pop-up box. The returned event object for both the date and the event selection AJAX behaviors contains the title, start date, end date, and all day properties:

```
public void onEventSelect(SelectEvent selectEvent) {
    event = (ScheduleEvent) selectEvent.getObject();
}

public void onDateSelect(SelectEvent selectEvent) {
    event = new DefaultScheduleEvent("", (Date)
    selectEvent.getObject(),(Date) selectEvent.getObject());
}
```

The returned event object from the preceding listener methods will be accessed by the `dialog` component to display the properties.

Click on the currently selected date. The event details in an editable format will be displayed, as follows:

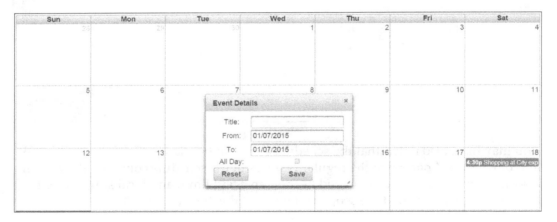

Clicking on the existing schedule event will display the event details in an editable format, as follows:

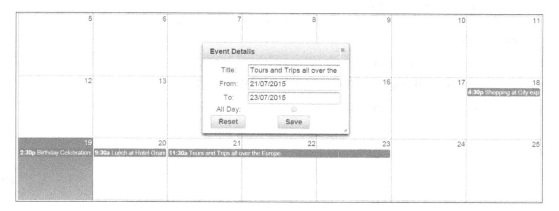

From the preceding screenshots, we can clearly see that PrimeFaces doesn't provide default skinning support for the selected date or an event which exists in the given range of dates. This makes the user try to manually create custom skinning support on the missing background color or to highlight the behavior required over the last user selection. That is, the background color change makes it easy for the user to read the text written over the schedule cell and remember the last user interaction.

Since there is no standard theme CSS rule that exists for the background color of a schedule cell, you need to go with dynamic changes from plain JS and CSS technologies.

Creating a CSS rule to set the background color in an HTML element

Before discussing how to apply background colors for the schedule component cells, let's create two pages, named `dynamicChangesClientsidecall.xhtml` and `dynamicChangesServersidecall.xhtml`, for both client-side and server-side approaches, respectively.

Before applying a CSS rule to set the background color for an HTML element, we first have to create a CSS class with the background color property .You can either add a CSS rule in the head section of the same XHTML file or in a separate external style sheet file. In this case, we are going to add the CSS rule in the same file for simplicity.

Add the following CSS style classes to both of the pages for date and event selection in the head section using the Facelets technology, as follows:

```
<ui:define name="name">
<style type="text/css">
  .scheduleDateBackground {
  background: yellow !important;
  }
</style>
<style type="text/css">
  .scheduleEventBackground {
  background: green !important;
  }
</style>
</ui:define>
```

Alternatively, you can add these CSS classes in the `default.css` file as an external style sheet.

These classes are going to be added to the schedule component with the help of JavaScript and jQuery code in the next section. There are no limitations on the number of styles that can be applied to a single HTML element. It is up to the customer requirements when it comes to enhancing the component's look and feel.

Creating a JavaScript function to apply CSS rules to a specific HTML element

It is not enough to create a CSS rule in order to apply skinning capabilities to an HTML element. We need to assign this CSS rule for a generated HTML element with the help of a JS function. If you look at the generated HTML for a schedule component using developer tools, then it clearly shows that each day cell in the schedule is a `<td>` element with a `data-date` attribute to store the current date.

The generated HTML for the schedule component of the first row will be as follows:

```
▼<div class="fc-day-grid-container fc-scroller" style="height: 5px;">
  ▼<div class="fc-day-grid">
    ▼<div class="fc-row fc-week ui-widget-content" style>
      ▼<div class="fc-bg">
        ▼<table>
          ▼<tbody>
            ▼<tr>
                <td class="fc-day ui-widget-content fc-sun fc-other-month fc-past" data-date="2015-06-28"></td>
                <td class="fc-day ui-widget-content fc-mon fc-other-month fc-past" data-date="2015-06-29"></td>
                <td class="fc-day ui-widget-content fc-tue fc-other-month fc-past" data-date="2015-06-30"></td>
                <td class="fc-day ui-widget-content fc-wed fc-past" data-date="2015-07-01"></td>
                <td class="fc-day ui-widget-content fc-thu fc-past" data-date="2015-07-02"></td>
                <td class="fc-day ui-widget-content fc-fri fc-past" data-date="2015-07-03"></td>
                <td class="fc-day ui-widget-content fc-sat fc-past" data-date="2015-07-04"></td>
            </tr>
          </tbody>
        </table>
      </div>
    ▼<div class="fc-content-skeleton">
      ▼<table>
        ▼<thead>
          ▼<tr>
              <td class="fc-day-number fc-sun fc-other-month fc-past" data-date="2015-06-28">28</td>
              <td class="fc-day-number fc-mon fc-other-month fc-past" data-date="2015-06-29">29</td>
              <td class="fc-day-number fc-tue fc-other-month fc-past" data-date="2015-06-30">30</td>
              <td class="fc-day-number fc-wed fc-past" data-date="2015-07-01">1</td>
              <td class="fc-day-number fc-thu fc-past" data-date="2015-07-02">2</td>
              <td class="fc-day-number fc-fri fc-past" data-date="2015-07-03">3</td>
              <td class="fc-day-number fc-sat fc-past" data-date="2015-07-04">4</td>
          </tr>
        </thead>
        ▼<tbody>
          ▼<tr>
              <td></td>
              <td></td>
              <td></td>
              <td></td>
```

Now, let's create a JS function in the head section for the yellow background color required for the date selection. The JavaScript function is created in two ways, based on either client-side or server-side access.

The client-side access approach to set the background color for a selected date can be implemented by adding the following code snippet in the head tag of the dynamicChangesClientsidecall.xhtml page:

```
function setSelectedDateBackground() {
  var selecteddate = document.getElementById
    ('mainForm:currentdate').value;
  $('.scheduleDateBackground').removeClass
    ('scheduleDateBackground');
  $('td[data-date=' + selecteddate +
    ']').addClass('scheduleDateBackground');
}
```

The server-side access approach to set the background color for a selected date can be implemented by adding the following code snippet in the head tag of the dynamicChangesServersidecall.xhtml page:

```
function setSelectedDateBackground(selecteddate) {
  $('.scheduleDateBackground').removeClass
    ('scheduleDateBackground');
  $('td[data-date=' + selecteddate + ']').addClass
    ('scheduleDateBackground');
}
```

After doing this, create another JS function in the head section of the green background color for event selection in the date range. The JavaScript function is created in two ways, based on either client-side or server-side access.

The client-side access approach to set the background color for a selected event can be implemented by adding the following code snippet in the head tag of the dynamicChangesClientsidecall.xhtml page:

```
function setSelectedEventBackground() {
  var startdate = document.getElementById
    ('mainForm:startdate').value;
  var enddate = document.getElementById('mainForm:enddate').value;
  $('.scheduleEventBackground').removeClass
    ('scheduleEventBackground');

  var startdate = new Date(startdate);
  var enddate = new Date(enddate);
  while (startdate <= enddate) {
    var currentdate = startdate;
    $('td[data-date=' + currentdate.toISOString().substr(0,10) +
      ']').addClass('scheduleEventBackground');
      startdate.setDate(startdate.getDate() + 1);
  }
}
```

The server-side access approach to set the background color for a selected event can be implemented by adding the following code snippet in the head tag of the dynamicChangesServersidecall.xhtml page:

```
function setSelectedEventBackground(startdate, enddate) {
  $('.scheduleDateBackground').removeClass
    ('scheduleDateBackground');
```

```
var startdate = new Date(startdate);
var enddate = new Date(enddate);

while (startdate <= enddate) {
  var currentdate = startdate;
  $('td[data-date=' + currentdate.toISOString().substr(0,10) +
    ']').addClass('scheduleDateBackground');
  startdate.setDate(startdate.getDate() + 1);
  }
}
```

In the preceding JS functions, we cleared the previous schedule date background before performing a new date or event selection. You will see how JS functions are invoked from the client-side or server-side in the next section.

Executing a client-side JavaScript function from the server-side – the power of AJAX and RequestContext

In the previous sections, we have created a CSS rule and a JS function to apply a background color to an HTML element. The JS function needs to be executed by a JS function call when either date selection or event selection AJAX events get fired. We need to pass the currently selected date as an argument for the date selection JS function and the start date and end date as arguments for the event selection JS function.

In this case (a plain JSF application approach), we will generally store the listener arguments in hidden input variables and update those values on the AJAX update. Then we will create JS functions to retrieve the date arguments from DOM and apply the background color for the schedule date cells. These JS functions need to be executed from the oncomplete JS callbacks of the AJAX requests. This is the first approach for applying date and event background colors to a schedule component.

Let's first write down the hidden variables to store all the date arguments in the dynamicChangesClientsidecall.xhtml file, as follows:

```
<h:inputHidden id="startdate"
  value="#{myScheduleView.startDate}"/>
<h:inputHidden id="enddate" value="#{myScheduleView.endDate}"/>
<h:inputHidden id="currentdate"
  value="#{myScheduleView.currentDate}"/>
```

The schedule AJAX event calls will update the date arguments through the update attribute and the JS functions are executed from the `oncomplete` callbacks, as follows:

```
<p:ajax event="dateSelect" listener=
  "#{myScheduleView.onDateSelectForCurrentdate}"
  update="eventDetails,currentdate"
  oncomplete="setSelectedDateBackground();
  PF('eventDialog').show();" />
<p:ajax event="eventSelect" listener=
  "#{myScheduleView.onEventSelectForDaterange}"
  update="eventDetails,startdate,enddate"
  oncomplete="setSelectedEventBackground();
  PF('eventDialog').show();" />
```

After doing this, we need to create listener methods and date properties in the backing Bean (`MyScheduleView.java`) to access them on the client-side:

```
SimpleDateFormat sdf = null;
String startDate = null;
String endDate = null;
String currentDate = null;

public void onDateSelectForCurrentdate(SelectEvent selectEvent) {
   event = new DefaultScheduleEvent("", (Date)
     selectEvent.getObject(),
     (Date) selectEvent.getObject());
     currentDate = sdf.format(event.getStartDate());
}
public void onEventSelectForDaterange(SelectEvent selectEvent) {
   event = (ScheduleEvent) selectEvent.getObject();
   startDate = sdf.format(event.getStartDate());
   endDate = sdf.format(event.getEndDate());
}
// Getters and Setters
```

Now, in the XHTML file, the date properties are retrieved by the client-side JS functions to apply the background colors for the cells as follows. Please refer to the usage of these variables in the JS functions, as defined in the previous section:

```
var selecteddate=
  document.getElementById('mainForm:currentdate').value;
var startdate =
  document.getElementById('mainForm:startdate').value;
var enddate = document.getElementById('mainForm:enddate').value;
```

The entire aforementioned approach is available in the `dynamicChangesClientsidecall.xhtml` page from the `chapter7` menu section.

Fortunately, PrimeFaces makes this task easier through the creation of the
`RequestContext` utility API methods. This is the second approach for applying
date and event background colors.

`RequestContext` is a simple utility that provides useful features, such as the
following:

- It executes a script after the AJAX request completes or during a page load
- It updates components programmatically
- It adds AJAX callback parameters as JSON
- Scroll to the component with a given client ID after an AJAX
  request completes
- It identifies the request as either an AJAX or a non-AJAX request

In this case, we will use the `RequestContext` utility to execute the script after an
AJAX request is fired. The `dateSelect` event listener method accepts `SelectEvent`
as an argument from which you can retrieve the `scheduleEvent` and the selected
schedule date. Then we can use an `execute` method of `RequestContext` for client-
side JS function invocation with the selected date as an argument, as follows:

```
public void onDateSelectBackgroundSelectEvent selectEvent) {
    event = new DefaultScheduleEvent("", (Date)
      selectEvent.getObject(),
      (Date) selectEvent.getObject());

    SimpleDateFormat sdf = new SimpleDateFormat("yyyy-MM-dd");
    Date date = (Date) event.getStartDate();
    String dateCell = sdf.format(date);
    RequestContext.getCurrentInstance().execute(
      String.format("setSelectedDateBackground('%s');", dateCell));
}
```

Similarly, the `eventSelect` method accepts `SelectEvent` as an argument from
which you can retrieve `ScheduleEvent` along with the start date and end date of the
schedule event. In this case, we should pass both the start date and end date for the
JS function, as follows:

```
public void onEventSelectBackground (SelectEvent selectEvent) {
    event = (ScheduleEvent) selectEvent.getObject();

    SimpleDateFormat sdf = new SimpleDateFormat("yyyy-MM-dd");
    Date startDate = event.getStartDate();
    Date endDate = event.getEndDate();
    String startDateCell = sdf.format(startDate);
```

```
String endDateCell = sdf.format(endDate);
RequestContext.getCurrentInstance().execute(
String.format("setSelectedEventBackground('%s','%s');",
  startDateCell, endDateCell));
}
```

Now run the application and navigate to the newly created page
(the `dynamicChangesServersidecall` page from the `chapter7` menu) and
you should see the background color applied to the currently selected date,
as shown in the following screenshot:

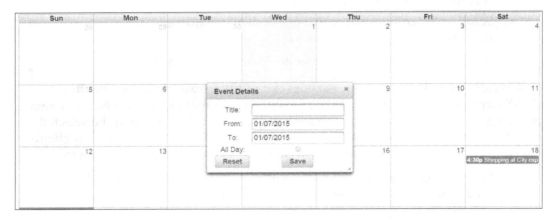

Note the yellow background applied to the selected date. Remember that each
previously selected date's background will be erased after the new date is selected.

However, the background color applied to a schedule event selected spans across a
date range, as shown in the following screenshot:

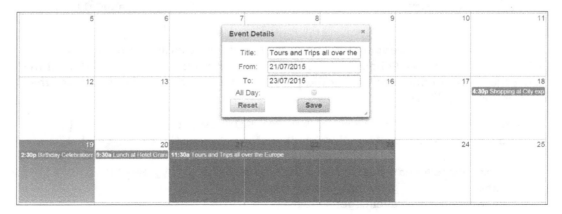

Note the green background applied to the date range of the selected event. Remember that each previously selected event's background will be erased after the new event is selected.

This way you can change a PrimeFaces component's look and feel with dynamic changes, depending on the state of the underlying data.

Summary

In this chapter, we have explored ways to enhance a PrimeFaces component's look and feel based on the state of the underlying data apart from the theme and what this can do. We've had a look at the schedule component and its features, the problem with the currently selected date or schedule event, and how to create a CSS rule to change the background color of an HTML element, and then how to execute the JavaScript function to apply a CSS rule to an HTML element. Finally, we have learned how to execute a JavaScript function when a schedule date is selected without JavaScript by just using the AJAX and `RequestContext` PrimeFaces utilities API. All the aforementioned topics were explained with a schedule example. Now that you have reached the end of this chapter, you should be comfortable using dynamic changes using JavaScript, CSS, AJAX, and `RequestContext` of PrimeFaces API on PrimeFaces components.

In the next chapter, we are going to discover how PrimeFaces Mobile is used for mobile web apps and how to ensure that your theme is suitable for mobile applications.

8
Mobile Web Apps

In this chapter, we will look at PrimeFaces Mobile and learn how to create customized mobile themes using ThemeRoller and apply a customized mobile theme that is suitable for mobile web applications.

In this chapter, we will cover the following topics:

- The demand of creating a powerful mobile website
- Restrictions of real estate – mobile device screens are simply smaller
- Introducing PrimeFaces Mobile for JSF-based applications
- Differences between PrimeFaces Mobile and the *normal* PrimeFaces
- Creating customized mobile themes – the power of jQuery Mobile ThemeRoller
- Applying customized mobile themes for PrimeFaces Mobile

The demand of creating a powerful mobile website

These days, mobile web traffic is dramatically on the rise, and creating a mobile-friendly experience is on everyone's mind. Having a mobile website is no longer a nice-to-have thing but a necessity, considering the latest trends. Even with slower networks, users might expect an application with quick navigation, a smooth loading experience, animated transitions, a responsive design, and so on.

In a mobile world, there are three types of modern apps—mobile web apps, native applications, and hybrid applications. The type of application that you need to choose to develop mobile software totally depends on the audience and target platform. If you already have a website and want to have a companion app or expand the app market, then it is better to start creating a mobile-friendly website (or web app). The main advantage of creating mobile web apps is that they are scalable and easy to create and maintain and they support multiple target platforms.

The most common misconception that I've heard about mobile websites is that they are just smaller versions of their desktop websites. But this is not true. If you try to open desktop websites using a smartphone, then you will clearly see that an illegible version of a regular website appears with cumbersome graphics and a bad navigation experience. A mobile website is specially designed and scaled for smaller screen sizes. Some of the features of mobile web apps that distinguish them from desktop websites are as follows:

- They are easy to read and have quick up-front menu navigation buttons
- A click-to-call feature to dial a number with a touch of your finger
- GPS or directions feature to find out a location quickly without typing anything
- All the menus, buttons, and popups are designed for easy and fast loading of a page on networks and hardware with slower connections

Considering this demand or benefits of mobile web apps, the PrimeFaces team created a mobile version of the PrimeFaces project.

Restrictions of real estate mobile device screens are simply smaller

By necessity, mobile screens are small because a mobile phone has to fit into a person's pocket or purse. The small size of mobile screens limits the controls and amount of the content that appear on them. So, there is an obvious change in the user experience between desktop web and mobile web interactions.

The smaller screens on touch devices reduce the context, which makes it difficult for users to find an overview of the page, the various options that are available, and remember prior content on the page. It also causes inaccurate clicks and error-prone typing.

Let's consider a page with a long form having various inputs and buttons. When a user scrolls down the page, the title of the page and previously entered data will disappear from the viewport. Without this information (or context), it is very difficult to get the meaning of the currently visible fields. So in this instance, we can have an overview or the title of the page as a fixed header during the page scroll.

Hence, mobile sites need to be designed with clickable elements that are large enough, keeping the page content shorter and the font sizes larger. They should also have features such as a confirmation popup to prevent accidental clicks, an "undo" feature to revert accidental behavior, the preselecting of default form fields, a responsive navigation system, transitions and effects, and so on.

Therefore, these limitations and recommendations need to be taken care of to develop a powerful mobile web app.

Introducing PrimeFaces Mobile for JSF-based applications

The PrimeFaces team introduced the PrimeFaces Mobile project after considering the demand from the community and mobile market. Initially, it started as a separate project and continued being developed until version 0.9.4, which came with fewer components in a single JAR file. Later, the PrimeFaces team decided to merge the mobile version with the core PrimeFaces itself. The reason behind this decision is that compatibility issues arose when using the two different libraries. In PrimeFaces 5.0, the mobile version is merged with the core and reloaded with features such as Mobile RenderKit for PrimeFaces components, an integrated navigation model, mobile AJAX behavior events, AJAX framework extensions, the lazy loading of pages, responsive widgets, and so on.

PrimeFaces Mobile is a UI kit built on top of jQuery Mobile (a touch-optimized HTML5 UI framework) to create JSF applications that are optimized for mobile devices. Some of its features are multiplatform support and PrimeFaces Mobile RenderKit for JSF and PrimeFaces components. It requires no installations on a device, the same backend model exists for both its desktop and mobile site, and AJAX behaviors are used to deliver native application experience.

Let's explore the basic setup and configurations required for a PrimeFaces Mobile application with a simple example.

As already mentioned, you are not required to download any library, because PrimeFaces Mobile API is shipped with PrimeFaces core API. At first glance, we need to configure the mobile-specific navigation handler inside the faces configuration, as follows:

```
<application>
  <navigation-handler>
    org.primefaces.mobile.application.MobileNavigationHandler
  </navigation-handler>
</application>
```

After this, in the same faces configuration (the `faces-config.xml` file), it is required to configure the Mobile RenderKit, which is specially created to optimize the component renderers for mobile environments:

```
<application>
  <default-render-kit-id>PRIMEFACES_MOBILE</default-render-kit-id>
</application>
```

The aforementioned global configuration is useful when the application is fully created with mobile pages. You can also apply the Mobile RenderKit for specific pages using the JSF core view tag as an alternative approach, as follows:

```
<f:view renderKitId="PRIMEFACES_MOBILE" />
```

The PFThemes project for this book is created as a desktop web application. So, we will follow the second approach to configure the mobile render kit.

The tag library for the PrimeFaces Mobile components is similar to the PrimeFaces `tag` library, as follows:

```
xmlns:pm="http://primefaces.org/mobile"
```

Now, let's create a file named `mobileindex.xhtml` page in a newly created folder named `chapter08` with mobile containers defined such as the `pm:page` elements. You can define multiple pages in the same view, where the first page is visible on page load, as follows:

```
<!DOCTYPE html>
<html xmlns="http://www.w3.org/1999/xhtml"
xmlns:h="http://java.sun.com/jsf/html"
xmlns:f="http://java.sun.com/jsf/core"
xmlns:p="http://primefaces.org/ui"
xmlns:pm="http://primefaces.org/mobile">
```

```
<f:view renderKitId="PRIMEFACES_MOBILE" />
<h:head>
</h:head>
<h:body>
  <pm:page id="first">
    <pm:header title="Main Page"></pm:header>
    <pm:content>
       <p:link outcome="pm:second?transition=flip" />
    </pm:content>
  </pm:page>
  <pm:page id="second">
    <pm:header title="Second Page">
       <f:facet name="left"><p:button value="Back"
       icon="back" ></f:facet>
    </pm:header>
    <pm:content style="text-align:center">Hello mobile
    world</pm:content>
  </pm:page>
</h:body>
</html>
```

Each page contains a header and content data, which are wrapped with the
<pm:head> and <pm:content> tags. The welcome page (or first page) contains a
submit link and clicking on the link from this page will take you to a second page
with the defined *flip* transition. Clicking on the link from the first page will take you
to a second page with the defined flip transition:

Now, clicking on the submit link will take you to the second page. You can also go
back to the first page by using the back button, which is defined in the header:

The two preceding pages are placed in the same XHTML view and the navigations between the two pages are handled by a special navigation handler, where the ID of the page is prepended to the `'pm:'` keyword, which results in multipage navigation.

The differences between PrimeFaces Mobile and normal PrimeFaces

If you have prior experience of using PrimeFaces with standard JSF projects, then it is very easy to develop PrimeFaces Mobile UI because there is not much difference between PrimeFaces and PrimeFaces Mobile when it comes to the architectural style and usage except for the fact that mobile components are optimized for mobile environments.

PrimeFaces Mobile depends on PrimeFaces core API, but it differs in a few areas. The following are some of the differences:

- PrimeFaces Mobile has its own render kit for mobile components
- The mobile version has a few separate resources, such as CSS, JS, and icons, along with ThemeRoller for custom themes
- PrimeFaces Mobile supports a subset of PrimeFaces components (or jQuery-based widgets) that are optimized for mobile devices
- A mobile project requires its own specific configuration, such as a navigation handler, render kit, a theme context parameter, and a tab library for mobile components

Let's demonstrate the difference between the look and feel of components of the PrimeFaces core API and PrimeFaces Mobile pages.

First, create the `primefacespage.xhtml` file (inside the `chapter8` folder) with the PrimeFaces core input and the `select` components:

```
<ui:composition template="././../WEB-
INF/resources/templates/chaptersTemplate.xhtml">
  <ui:define name="title">
    PrimeFaces registration
  </ui:define>
  <ui:define name="menu"></ui:define>
  <ui:define name="content">
    <h:form id="mainForm">
```

```
      <h:panelGrid columns="2">
        <h:outputText value="First Name: "></h:outputText>
        <p:inputText id="firstname" style="float:left"/>
        <h:outputText value="Last Name: "></h:outputText>
        <p:inputText id="lastname" style="float:left"/>
        <h:outputText value="Address: "></h:outputText>
        <p:inputTextarea id="address" style="float:left"/>
        <h:outputText value="Gender: " />>
        <p:selectOneRadio id="gender" value="Male">
          <f:selectItem itemLabel="Male" itemValue="Male" />
          <f:selectItem itemLabel="Female" itemValue="Female" />
        </p:selectOneRadio>
        <h:outputText value="Select City:" />
        <p:selectOneMenu id="city" value="#{weatherView.city}"
        style="float:left;width:200px">
          <f:selectItem itemLabel="India" itemValue="India" />
          <f:selectItem itemLabel="USA" itemValue="USA" />
          <f:selectItem itemLabel="UK" itemValue="UK" />
        </p:selectOneMenu>
        <h:outputText value="Qualification:" />
        <p:selectOneButton value="MTech">
          <f:selectItem itemLabel="MS" itemValue="MS" />
          <f:selectItem itemLabel="MTech" itemValue="MTech" />
          <f:selectItem itemLabel="PhD" itemValue="PhD" />
        </p:selectOneButton>
        <h:outputText value="Graduation percentage: " />
        <h:panelGroup>
          <h:inputText id="grade" value="50" />
          <p:slider for="grade" />
        </h:panelGroup>
        <h:outputText value="Disclaimer agreed: " />
        <h:selectBooleanCheckbox
        style="float:left;width:20px;height:20px" value="true"/>
        <h:outputText></h:outputText>
        <p:commandButton value="Submit"
        style="float:left"></p:commandButton>
      </h:panelGrid>
    </h:form>
  </ui:define>
</ui:composition>
```

Now, run the application and navigate to the newly created page, which looks like the following screenshot:

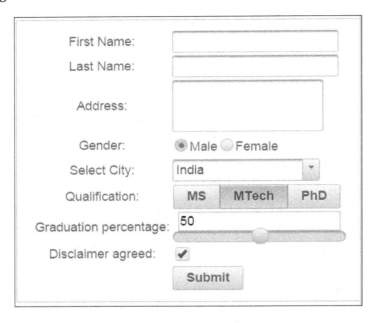

After this, create the `primefacesmobilepage.xhtml` file (inside the `chapter8` folder) with the `input` and `select` components that are the same as those of a PrimeFaces Mobile page, as follows:

```
<ui:composition template="././../WEB-
INF/resources/templates/mobileTemplate.xhtml">
  <ui:define name="title">
    PrimeFaces Mobile page
  </ui:define>
  <ui:define name="header">
    <pm:header title="Registration" fixed="true"/>
  </ui:define>
  <ui:define name="content">
    <pm:content>
      <pm:field>
        <p:outputLabel value="First Name: " />
        <p:inputText id="firstname" />
      </pm:field>
      <pm:field>
        <p:outputLabel value="Last Name: " />
```

```
          <p:inputText id="lastname" />
        </pm:field>
        <pm:field>
          <h:outputLabel value="Address: " />
          <p:inputTextarea id="address" rows="3" />
        </pm:field>
        <pm:field>
          <p:outputLabel for="gender" value="Gender: " />
          <p:selectOneRadio id="gender" value="Male">
            <f:selectItem itemLabel="Male" itemValue="Male" />
            <f:selectItem itemLabel="Female" itemValue="Female" />
          </p:selectOneRadio>
        </pm:field>
        <pm:field>
          <p:outputLabel for="city" value="Select City:" />
          <p:selectOneMenu id="city" value="India">
            <f:selectItem itemLabel="India" itemValue="India" />
            <f:selectItem itemLabel="USA" itemValue="USA" />
            <f:selectItem itemLabel="UK" itemValue="UK" />
          </p:selectOneMenu>
        </pm:field>
        <pm:field>
          <h:outputLabel value="Qualification:" />
          <p:selectOneButton value="MTech">
            <f:selectItem itemLabel="MS" itemValue="MS" />
            <f:selectItem itemLabel="MTech" itemValue="MTech" />
            <f:selectItem itemLabel="PhD" itemValue="PhD" />
          </p:selectOneButton>
        </pm:field>
        <pm:field>
          <p:outputLabel for="grade" value="Grade: " />
          <pm:inputSlider id="grade" value="50" />
        </pm:field>
        <pm:field>
          <h:outputLabel value="Disclaimer: " />
          <p:selectBooleanCheckbox value="true"
          itemLabel="I agree"/>
        </pm:field>
        <p:commandButton value="Submit"></p:commandButton>
      </pm:content>
    </ui:define>
    <ui:define name="footer"></ui:define>
  </ui:composition>
```

Now, run the application and navigate to the newly created page, which looks like the following screenshot:

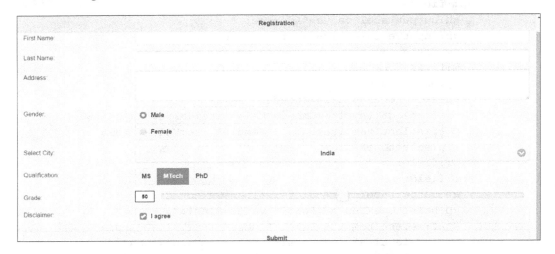

 Note that considering the size of the book, we are not going to add the entire code sections for `primefacespage.xhtml` and `primefacesmobilepage.xhtml`. The code is available in the `chapter8` section of the GitHub PFThemes Project (for more information, visit `https://github.com/andyba/PFThemes`).

From the preceding screenshots, it's clear that the form components in mobile pages are bigger than those of the desktop web browsers. This behavior is intentional, as this prevents inaccurate clicks in smaller mobile screens. Also, there will be changes in the font family, font size, text shadows, skinning, and so on. Even though we used core PrimeFaces components (most of the components in the page), the look and feel of widgets will change in mobile environments.

Creating customized mobile themes – the power of jQuery Mobile ThemeRoller

PrimeFaces Mobile themes are based on jQuery themes, which provide the CSS framework to give the necessary, consistent, and touch-friendly look and feel for widgets across all platforms.

Each theme contains multiple color schemes known as **swatches**. We use single-letter designations for swatches. You don't need to specify a swatch for each widget available in the page. By default, for most of the widgets, the theme option is set to null, which means that you can override the swatch for each individual widget. Because of the default null value, we can set the swatch for the outermost container. Then, the swatch will be inherited or applied to all the widgets inside the container.

The theme also defines the "active" state apart from all the swatches. The intention of this state is to give immediate feedback for a brief processing delay. jQuery Mobile adds the active state for a button once a user lifts their finger from the touchscreen and until the triggering of the click event, which takes a delay of 300 milliseconds in mobile devices.

The jQuery mobile theme framework provides up to 26 swatches starting from "a" to "z". The framework comes with five default swatches ("a" to "e"), which can be directly used or overwritten. If no theme swatch is defined, the default swatch mapping for components will be as follows:

- The framework uses the "a" swatch for headers and footers. The default theme uses the color black for the swatch.
- The "c" swatch is used for widget content to contrast with the "a" swatch. The default theme uses a light gray color for the swatch.
- The list dividers in list views, the header of the nested list pages, and the button of split button lists use the "b" swatch. The default theme uses the color blue for the swatch.
- The error messages use the "e" swatch. The default theme uses the color yellow for the swatch.
- The "d" swatch used as an alternate secondary color.

You can also configure the aforementioned colors globally and add new swatches where required. Every theme also includes a font family, drop shadows for overlays, and corner radio values for buttons and boxes.

We can also manually edit swatches in a default theme and add additional swatches by just copying the block of swatch styles and renaming their classes with new swatch names in the theme CSS file. But most changes can be done using ThemeRoller.

ThemeRoller is used to create custom themes, and each theme can be composed of up to a maximum of 26 swatches. The official site of jQuery Mobile ThemeRoller is available at `http://themeroller.jquerymobile.com/`.

First, we have to create our own swatch by using the drag-and-drop user interface. By default, it offers or showcases three swatches (a, b, and c) in the display (see the following screenshot). You can either use the default colors or the Adobe Kuler color, or create your own colors. The custom theme is created by dragging the color onto the selected element in the swatch. You can add new swatches by clicking on the plus (**+**) symbol from the menu to the left.

Let's choose the colors for elements of A swatch, as follows:

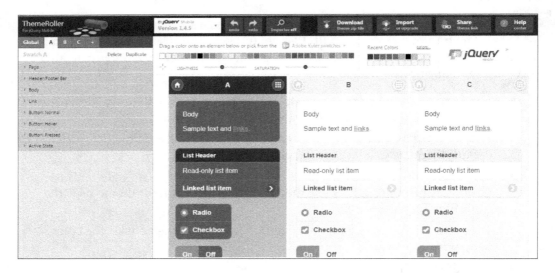

If required, you can further edit the swatch from the menu to the left. Expand the various elements' parts and modify the styles, such as the text color, text shadow size, position, gradient color, and so on, as follows:

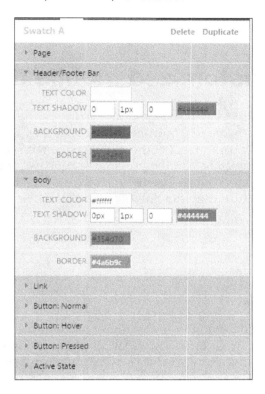

You can also add alternative icons by checking off the checkbox of the "show alternative icons in preview" button. The amount of CSS style changes that you can make for a custom theme purely depends on the requirement.

Now, it is time to download the jQuery Mobile theme as a ZIP file, which contains the themes folder along with index.html to test the skinning on a few widgets. The Themes folder will contain the images folder, the themes CSS file in a minimized and non-minimized version, and an icons CSS file in a minimized version, as follows:

By default, PrimeFaces Mobile API will add mobile icons and structural CSS styles (`jquery-mobile-icons.css` and `jquery-mobile-structure.css`) using its `HeaderRender.java` file in the `head` section of the generated HTML. So, we just need to carry out a custom theme CSS file and an `images` folder to apply the newly created theme to a PrimeFaces Mobile application.

Applying customized mobile themes to PrimeFaces Mobile

The default PrimeFaces theme (the built-in one) provides two swatches (a and b), but you can change the look and feel of the mobile page with custom themes that have their own various swatches. In the previous section, we saw how to create a custom theme using jQuery Mobile ThemeRoller. Now, it is time to create a JAR file with the following structure from the downloaded ZIP folder:

```
- jar
  -META-INF
    - resources
      - primefaces-customtheme
        - theme.css
        - images
```

Alternatively, you can add the `primefaces-customtheme` folder inside the resources folder of the current application. This approach is only used in the PFThemes project while applying PrimeFaces and PrimeFaces Mobile custom themes (that is, the ones named `moodyblue2` and `customtheme`).

Before using a custom theme, we need to perform a few modifications. This is just a two-step process:

1. Copy the custom theme into the `primefaces-customtheme` folder by renaming it `theme.css` and copying all images to the `images` folder.

2. Modify the image references in the `theme.css` file to an expression that the JSF resource loading will understand.

Once the theme is available in the class path, the custom theme can be enabled in the application using the following configuration:

```
<context-param>
  <param-name>primefaces.mobile.THEME</param-name>
  <param-value>customtheme</param-value>
</context-param>
```

 The mobile page requires customtheme context parameter setting in order to view the custom mobile theme on your components. Otherwise registration appears with default PrimeFaces theme.

The mobile page created in the previous section (named primefacesmobilepage.xhtml) in the desktop web browser will look like the following screenshot:

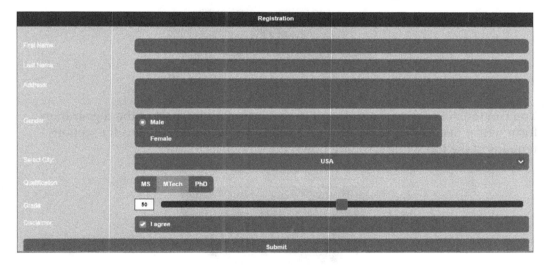

Testing mobile pages on desktop browsers won't give the exact results of a mobile environment, and testing on physical devices always pays off. In this case, you can use mobile emulators that enable you to test mobile websites in many cell phones or mobile devices with different models. These virtual environments not only expand your testing coverage to more devices, but also provide you with a quick and easy way to test small changes on the fly.

Let's test mobile pages on an Opera emulator with the dimensions of Samsung Galaxy S mobile device model:

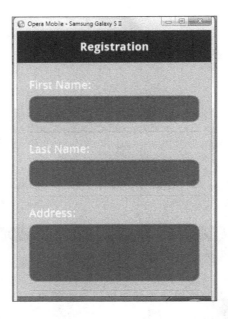

You can touch the screen and drag it to see the remaining part of the registration form with a fixed header. Because we added a fixed header, the header section remains at the top while scrolling down the screen, as follows:

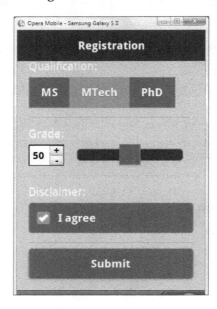

Apart from the preceding simple form input components, you can also test mobile pages that have complex widgets and change their style as required. You can style or customize the mobile themes which are well-suited for the mobile environment.

Summary

In this chapter, we explored the demand to create a powerful mobile website and the restrictions of mobile real estate considering their smaller screens. PrimeFaces Mobile for JSF-based applications was introduced. We learned the difference between core PrimeFaces and its mobile version, created customized mobile themes using jQuery Mobile ThemeRoller, and applied customized themes for PrimeFaces Mobile themes. All these topics were explained with proper examples. Now that you've reached the end of this chapter, you should be comfortable creating mobile web apps and applying customized themes to your application.

In the next chapter, we are going to learn how to ensure that our custom theme is complete by applying it to the PrimeFaces showcase and making component-specific skinning changes as required.

9
The Final Touches

As seen in *Chapters 2, Introducing PrimeFaces Themes* and *Chapter 3, jQuery UI, ThemeRoller, and the Anatomy of a Theme,* a theme is structured in such a way that every component inherits the look and feel of the generalized CSS rules while having rules specific to each component.

The easiest way to make sure that your theme is complete is by using the **PrimeFaces showcase** and applying your theme to it. You can then browse through the showcase and apply the common CSS rules and component-specific changes where appropriate. Details of the component-specific CSS rules can be found in the skinning section of each UI component description in the *PrimeFaces User Guide.*

In this chapter, we will cover the following topics:

- The PrimeFaces showcase
- See what you don't like and apply the changes
- See what you do like and make everything look that way
- Do the same for PrimeFaces Mobile
- Packaging your custom theme
- Creating CSS files that provide variations of a theme

The PrimeFaces showcase

In the previous chapters, we had a look at all the possible ways to make better use of themes and their benefits and flexibility in an optimal way. We also studied some well-explained examples. As you may already know, the PrimeFaces UI suite provides a big set of interactive widgets, and it is quite impossible to cover each component in this book.

The examples in this book took a few components that are suitable for the demonstration of the concepts in a clear manner with proper code snippets and screenshots. As a JSF or PrimeFaces developer, you may need to deal with a large number of components and their features. The CSS skinning will vary from component to component, and it is difficult to play with them by creating simple examples.

The official PrimeFaces user guide (this user guide is available in the **User Guides** section of the PrimeFaces documentation for each PrimeFaces release and can be viewed by visiting `http://www.primefaces.org/documentation`) covers component tags, attributes, features, events, and most importantly, component-specific CSS rules in the skinning section of each component. Apart from this helpful documentation, the PrimeFaces team also created a demo application to demonstrate each component and its features with the best examples known as showcase application. The showcase is constructed in such a way that all the related components are present in one group.

The latest PrimeFaces showcase is deployed on the Jetty server and is available at `http://primefaces.org/showcase/`.

You can also either check out the source code of the showcase application from the GitHub link, or download the deployable version of the showcase application locally for more control.

The GitHub showcase project and the downloadable version of showcase war is available at the following links:

- The source code of the PrimeFaces showcase in the following GitHub URL link:

    `https://github.com/primefaces/showcase`

- The showcase war files for each PrimeFaces versions are available at the following URL:

    `http://www.primefaces.org/downloads`

 The **showcase war project** files are added from the PrimeFaces 5.0 release and onwards in their community releases.

Perform the following steps to build the showcase source locally:

1. Clone the GitHub repository in your local filesystem and import the showcase project into the workspace, as follows:

   ```
   git clone https://github.com/primefaces/showcase.git
   ```

2. Clean your cached output from the target folder, as follows:

   ```
   mvn clean
   ```

3. Create a war file in the target folder by using the following command:

   ```
   mvn package
   ```

4. Run the showcase project (showcase application uses **jetty** plugin as a web server), as follows:

   ```
   mvn jetty:run
   ```

Now, you can access the deployed PrimeFaces showcase by entering `http://localhost:8080/showcase/` URL in your browser:

A search menu on the left-hand side of the showcase site has the listed components which are all related placed in one group. A click on each component shows the demo example for each feature.

It is time to add the custom theme (moodyblue2) that was created in the previous chapters in the showcase resources folder. Then, add the theme name in the ThemeService.java file to select a custom theme from the ThemeSwitcher component. You can immediately find the theme applied on the PrimeFaces widget components in the current page.

However, in order to reflect the `moodyblue2` theme on all the PrimeFaces components (or all the pages) in the showcase project, we will replace the `primefaces.THEME` dynamic EL with the `moodyblue2` in `web.xml` file, as follows:

```
<context-param>
   <param-name>primefaces.THEME</param-name>
   <param-value>moodyblue2</param-value>
</context-param>
```

For a quick reference, the showcase also provides an example code of each component feature at the bottom of the page and also an user guide in the **Documentation** tab next to the code section.

See what you don't like in the showcase and apply the changes

In the previous chapters, we saw how to create themes according to customer requirements using the ThemeRoller framework and also how to customize the theme by manually editing the CSS properties of the `theme.css` file. But in this chapter, you are going to learn how to customize themes by installing the existing theme (`moodyblue2` as an example) on the showcase application and then making changes to the aspects of the theme that you don't like.

These days, designers use the *rounded corners* feature frequently because they are industry standards more than a design trend. Some expert says that rectangles with rounded corners are easier on the eyes than a rectangle with sharp edges because less cognitive effort is required to visually process them. Considering this fact, by default, themes contain 3px rounded corners on every side of an HTML component.

However, you may think that it looks better to have a more rounding value on the corners. So now, debug the showcase page (`messages.xhtml`), which contains the `inputText` elements, using browser developer tools (by pressing *F12*). Change the rounded corner property to random values. You will see that each widget looks good with a moderate 5px value on each corner.

After changing the rounded corner value using developer tools, the input components will be as follows:

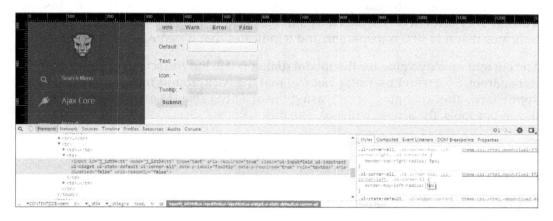

Now, apply the same CSS changes for the border radius in the `moodyblue2` theme, as follows:

```css
/* Corner radius */
.ui-corner-all,
.ui-corner-top,
.ui-corner-left,
.ui-corner-tl {
  border-top-left-radius: 5px;
}
.ui-corner-all,
.ui-corner-top,
.ui-corner-right,
.ui-corner-tr {
  border-top-right-radius: 5px;
}
.ui-corner-all,
.ui-corner-bottom,
.ui-corner-left,
.ui-corner-bl {
  border-bottom-left-radius: 5px;
}
.ui-corner-all,
.ui-corner-bottom,
.ui-corner-right,
.ui-corner-br {
  border-bottom-right-radius: 5px;
}
```

Now, we will move on to the other required CSS changes in the showcase application. In modal dialogs, you may have observed that a black shadow is applied to the background of the dialog to avoid user interactions. The **opacity** describes the transparency level, where 1 indicates that the background is not at all transparent, 0.5 indicates that it is 50% transparent, and 0 indicates that it's completely transparent.

The current opacity value for the modal dialog is 0.3, but the screen appears a bit transparent. So, an end user may not feel that the background transparency is applied. So, after changing or increasing the opacity value (to 0.4) by using the developer tools, the screen will look like this:

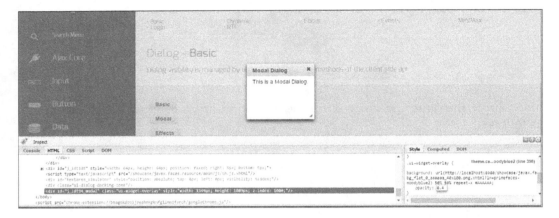

Internet Explorer 8 (IE8) and its earlier versions support an alternative—the filter property. In this case, the `filter` property should be defined as follows:

```
filter: Alpha (Opacity=40);
```

After doing this, we need to add the same CSS changes in the `theme.css` file to reflect our requirements in the PrimeFaces application, as follows:

```css
/* Overlays */
.ui-widget-overlay {
  background: #aaaaaa url("#{resource['primefaces-
    moodyblue2:images/ui-bg_flat_0_aaaaaa_40x100.png']}") 50% 50%
    repeat-x;
  opacity: .4;
  filter: Alpha(Opacity=40);
}
```

Also, the labels are dark black in color. So, let's modify the color from `#222222` to `#524545` in order to change the color to a lighter one for the output label text, as follows:

```
label.ui-outputlabel {
  color:#524545;
}
```

This way, you can browse each page and component of the showcase demo application and change the CSS properties as per your requirements.

See what you do like in the showcase and make everything look that way

In this section, we will customize the theme on the basis of what we do like about a specific theme's CSS feature in the showcase and make everything look that way by adding the same change.

In the previous chapters, while customizing themes, we added the regular `Segoe UI` font family for some component categories such as `input`, `select`, `textArea`, `button`, and so on. After this change, the font style looks more prominent, stylish, and readable. So, we would like to apply the same change to all the widgets of PrimeFaces.

The `Segoe UI` font family of the aforementioned component groups in the `theme.css` files, as follows:

```
.ui-widget input,
.ui-widget select,
.ui-widget textarea,
.ui-widget button {
  font-family: 'Segoe UI',Arial,sans-serif;
}
```

Let's add the same `font-family` attribute to the common CSS class named `.ui-widget`. Currently, the widget class supports the `Arial, sans-serif` font family by default, as follows:

```
.ui-widget {
  font-family: Arial,sans-serif;
  font-size: 1.0em;
}
```

After this, the following modified CSS is applied to all the widgets in the PrimeFaces component suite:

```
.ui-widget {
  font-family: 'Segoe UI'Arial,sans-serif;
  font-size: 1.0em;
}
```

Now, you can find the difference in the `font-family` attribute of all the widgets. The page now looks like the following screenshot:

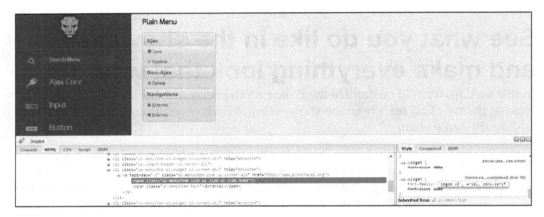

The developer tools can show the difference between the old and new font families by changing them instantly.

Do the changes same way for PrimeFaces Mobile

The aforementioned theme changes are not just specific to the desktop or PrimeFaces core themes. They can be applied to mobile themes as well. You can make changes to themes when you don't like a specific skinning feature. At the same time, you can follow similar skinning process across all the widgets when you like it.

For example, you will see how the `font-family`, `font-size`, and `line-height` CSS properties of a theme file are changed according to users' interests or requirements.

The default `font-family` attribute used by mobile themes is `sans-serif`. Let's try to change the `font-family` attribute to the newly added `RobotoRegular`, which is a `sans-serif` family developed by Google for the Android operating system. After doing this, increase the `font-size` value and decrease the `line-height` value a little for a better appearance and readability.

The preceding changes that were made to the CSS class and which were applied to the `body`, `input`, `select`, `textarea`, and `button` elements with the help of developer tools will look like this:

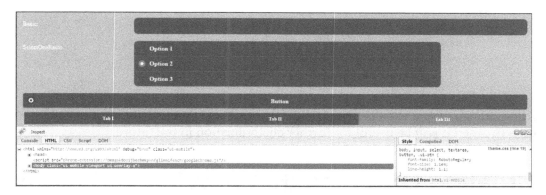

Copy the CSS property changes from the developer tools to the mobile theme (`theme.css`), as follows:

```
body,
input,select,textarea,button,
.ui-btn {
  font-size: 1.1em;
  line-height: 1.1;
  font-family: RobotoRegular /*{global-font-family}*/;
}
```

In the same manner, you can apply the mobile theme changes by browsing each page and each component of the showcase demo mobile section. The showcase will be redirected to the mobile showcase once you click on the PFMobile icon at the top of the showcase page.

Packaging your custom theme

As discussed in the previous chapters, once a theme is ready with all the custom changes, it can either be packaged as a JAR file, or we can add the `primefaces-moodyblue2` theme's distribution folder inside the `resources` folder of your web application.

The JAR file must have the following folder structure to work with the PrimeFaces infrastructure:

```
- jar
  -META-INF
    - resources
      - primefaces-moodyblue2
        - theme.css
        - images
```

Alternatively, if you use the `primefaces-moodyblue2` theme's distribution folder directly, then it will be useful for further customization in the future.

Creating CSS files that provide variations on a theme

In the previous sections, you saw that theme customization directly worked on the `theme.css` file of the PrimeFaces themes. You can also add the same customizations in an external CSS file and add it after the PrimeFaces registered theme file. For this purpose, you need to follow the **customizable resource ordering** concept.

PrimeFaces `HeaderRenderer` class implements the resource order as follows:

```
- "first" facet if defined
- Theme CSS
- "middle" facet if defined
- PF-JSF registered CSS and JS
- Head content
- "last" facet if defined
```

You can define a custom CSS file that contains all the aforementioned changes in the last facet to override the default theme CSS file. If you don't want to apply the changes to all the components, then add a namespace label before the CSS class name so that it can be applied to specific components.

For example, let's assume that the overridden CSS classes are added to an external file named `customstyle.css` and placed in the last facet, as follows:

```
<h:head>
  <f:facet name="first">
  </f:facet>
</h:head>
<h:body>
  <f:facet name="last">
  <h:outputStylesheet library="default"
    name="css/customstyle.css"/>
  </f:facet>
</h:body>
```

In the generated HTML, you can clearly see that the external file is added after the default theme file to override the style classes:

```
<link type="text/css" rel="stylesheet"
  href="/PFThemes/javax.faces.resource/primefaces.css.jsf?
  ln=primefaces"/>
<!-- comment : "last" faces -->
<link type="text/css" rel="stylesheet"
  href="/PFThemes/javax.faces.resource/css/customstyle.css.jsf?
  ln=default"/>
```

This way, the showcase demo application is very helpful in real-time theme development for practical purposes if you wish to customize theme CSS files instantly according to users' interests and requirements. You can use your browser's developer tools or firebug add-ons to obtain a screen preview for every theme CSS property change.

Summary

In this chapter, we discussed how the PrimeFaces showcase is useful for practical purposes in real-time theme development. We also learned how to build and run the showcase project, explored what we don't like and applied the required changes, and explored what we do like and made everything look similar in the project. After making changes to the existing theme, we had a look at how to package a custom theme. Finally, we created CSS files to provide variations of the theme.

In the next chapter, we are going to discuss best practices in theme development as well as the various best practices that are categorized into common web design, rich internet applications and finally, PrimeFaces themes.

Theme Design Best Practices **10**

In this chapter, we will look at best practices that need to be followed in theme development. We will also look at generally applicable best practices in web design as well as those in rich Internet applications and PrimeFaces themes.

In this chapter, we will cover the following best practices in theme development:

- An introduction to web WAI guidelines for good web design
- Colors, icon sets, background, and foreground
- Fonts make the text stand out
- Rich Internet applications versus desktop applications
- Functions per page
- Components that you will be using
- Some important PrimeFaces CSS classes
- Going beyond the standard built-in PrimeFaces theme
- Overriding the PrimeFaces CSS classes
- Overriding specific component CSS styles
- Previewing theme styles before using them
- Considerations for mobile applications
- Busy UI versus data-dominated UI
- Feedback from potential users
- Miscellaneous best practices

Introduction of WAI for good web design

Before discussing best practices of a theme, we will look at the official guidelines provided by the **World Wide Web Consortium (W3C)** for good web design. The **Web Accessibility Initiative (WAI)** of W3C is a set of guidelines intended for web developers and designers on how to improve web accessibility for people with disabilities. These guidelines are helpful not only for people with a disability, but also for users who work in difficult environments (such as strong light, darkness, bad light, and so on).

Some guidelines to improve web accessibility for a majority of users is as follows:

- Avoid poor color contrast to improve readability. Normally, black text on a white background or white text on a black background is suitable for all users. Make sure that you choose the right color contrast before designing a website.

- Use the `alt` attribute, which provides alternative text to an image. This is helpful when a user has turned off the display of images, mini browser, and voice browser.

- Don't use smaller fonts with small text size to increase the content space in a web page and squeezing the text.

- Always avoid fancy fonts. Normal fonts are easy to read, whereas fancy fonts such as the `Italic` and `Serif` fonts are difficult to read.

- Choose the best letter- and line-spacing properties for text content. Text with extra letter-spacing and a good line-spacing makes it easy to read it.

The advantages of making your website more accessible are as follows:

- This improves customer satisfaction and the reputation/brand value
- This also increases the number of visitors
- It makes your site more usable for old equipment
- Visitors stay for a longer span of time on your site

In this way, the WAI guidelines improve user accessibility for your website.

Colors, icon sets, background, and foreground

Colors are the visual perceptual property that correspond in humans to the categories called red, green, blue, yellow, and so on. The use of color to indicate an arbitrary object/property state must be intuitive, or you will need to provide a color key to go with it. A color is a tricky thing, and you have to use it in the right way, at the right time, with the right target audience, and for the right purpose. Otherwise, a web design can go wrong with too much color, mismatched color schemes, and too many interactive features.

Around the globe, 12% of the population has some form of color-vision deficiency (or color blindness). Therefore, the color scheme or harmony is a very important criterion when selecting the colors. It is recommended that you use a limited number of colors and try to avoid pure primary colors too much, which really dominate in the web design. It is good and sufficient to design a well-balanced website with three to four colors along with regular white and black colors. Too many colors will clash and distract users.

As you already know, a picture is worth a thousand words. It is recommended that you use small images to optimize the website and convey more information and use actual functionality. Icons will do the same thing. They are helpful if you wish to reduce the real estate of a website that is significantly occupied by, say, buttons. Also, by using image sprite (a set of icons as a single image) technology, a website's performance improves due to a reduction in the number of HTTP requests.

The foreground and background colors should be contrast well with each other as much as possible. Otherwise, it becomes difficult to read the text and see the icons. The contrast is simply just how bright a color is as compared to the background. If it is difficult to identify good color contrast combinations of foreground and background colors, then you can find some really good websites that provide you with a list of good and poor color combinations. For example, if you create a web page with blue text on a black background, then web users or readers will get eyestrain very quickly.

Fonts make the text stand out

As you already know, CSS font properties define the font family, boldness, size, and style of the text. These font properties make the text stand out from the rest of the page. You need to make sure that the font properties are customized in a right direction. Otherwise, it makes the text unreadable.

Changing the font size is an easy way to provide visual hierarchy and emphasis to the web page. The larger the font size, the greater the emphasis is on that text as compared to other text elements. The headings and titles require big font sizes to emphasize them from the surrounding text. Many users feel that some themes make the components slightly too large for most applications. In that case, we can reduce the font size directly, as follows:

```
.ui-widget, .ui-widget .ui-widget {
  font-size: 90% !important;
}
```

At the same time, we shouldn't use small text size to squeeze more text into a web page. Otherwise, website visitors will be forced to enlarge the text every time they visit the page.

The `font-family` property also has a major role when it comes to emphasizing and making the text stand out. Regular or normal fonts make the text more readable. For example, the `sans-serif` font is easier to read online, whereas the `Serif, Italic` font makes it difficult to read the text. All the built-in PrimeFaces themes follow the `Arial, sans-serif` font family across all the components for better readability:

```
.ui-widget
{
  font-family: Arial,sans-serif;
}
```

The `font-weight` property defines how thick or thin characters in text should be displayed. Themes uses a `bold` value for all component headers, which makes the text stand out from the content section:

```
.ui-widget-header
{
  font-weight: bold;
}
```

Using very light or bold font weights will distract the users.

Rich Internet applications versus desktop applications

Traditional desktop applications are mainly characterized by a rich user experience and complex UIs (menus, multiple windows, multiple tabs, and so on) that run fast and are deployed locally on the end user's platform. But it is going to be problematic when you are going to install, set up, maintain, and access it across networks with various security constraints on compatible hardware, OS, libraries, and so on.

Web applications overcome these aforementioned problems by introducing thin client server architecture based on internet protocols. Web browsers send requests to the server and get a response to display the output without any installations and maintenance. But the main problem is that it requires server interaction and a static look all the time and it lacks a rich UI.

Rich Internet applications (RIA) bring the best out of each one of them, and these are the enhanced web applications that have the additional functionality of a client, which makes them more responsive to the user. They have features and functionalities that are similar to that of desktop applications. A rich Internet application is capable of delivering a rich experience to users. The richness of the application is enhanced by making software more natural, connected, alive, interactive, and responsive.

To create a RIA, many frameworks have been introduced until today, but those are all internally based on HTML, JavaScript, CSS, and AJAX technologies. Nowadays, themes have a vital role in RIAs' development. Themes will add skinning features, a unified look and feel, transitions, effects, rounded corners, responsiveness, and so on, to improve the user's experience. Hence, it has been adopted by many frameworks and external libraries.

Remember that Rich UI is costly in terms of performance. A Rich UI implies more impact on the page load time. For example, the PrimeFaces `inputText` component is an enhanced JSF `inputText` component with rich skinning UI features. You can clearly see that a big `dataTable` with a bunch of PrimeFaces `inputText` components takes more time to load a page than a `dataTable` with standard JSF `inputText` components as a sample test.

Functions per page

The best website design mainly depends on how you define application functionalities in an effective, flexible, and optimized way with respect to screen real estate. For a complex web application, you might encounter a large number of functionalities in a single page. Adjusting all the functionalities in a single page and trying to squeeze in the information makes the design clumsy and confusing.

Therefore, you need to make sure that each page is designed with limited functionalities with some relevant relationship between them. In the same way, it is good to limit the number of functionalities that one component can do.

For example, adding bulky information to multiple data containers (`dataTable`, `datalist`, `datagrid`, and so on) with multiple features (such as row selection, edit, and horizontal and vertical scrolls) makes it difficult for users to grab all the functionalities that are available at a time. Instead of displaying a lot of data with a scrollable feature, it is recommended that you use dialogs and master/detail relationship to make the application simple and easy to navigate for additional information.

Components you will be using

Generally, we will design an application with a set of use cases or functionalities. Each use case includes several actions and components to make it meaningful. It is recommended that you use suitable components for the functionality. Otherwise, the application will fail to convey the actual information to the user.

A good example of how to not do this is by using the `Accordion` components to provide sections of inputs. The wizard components are by far a better choice. The wizard component in registration applications fills in data using a step-by-step procedure with the previous and next buttons. In that case, you can also have a clear picture of what happened recently.

Some important PrimeFaces CSS classes

In PrimeFaces themes, you will find that both component-specific CSS classes as well as common CSS classes are used across the components. You can find the component-specific CSS classes in the skinning section of each component in the PrimeFaces user guide.

Some of the most important PrimeFaces CSS classes that are used to customize the PrimeFaces theme are given in the following lines. They are grouped into certain CSS groups based on their purpose.

The widgets or components for container-specific CSS classes are as follows:

- `.ui-widget`: It can be applied to the outer container of all PrimeFaces components or widgets. It adds font-family and font size to widgets.
- `.ui-widget-header`: This is applied to the header section of a component.
- `.ui-widget-content`: This class can be applied to the content section of a component.

The interaction state CSS classes of a widget or component are as follows:

- `.ui-corner-all`: This adds rounded corners to HTML elements
- `.ui-state-default`: CSS applies to clickable button-like elements to represent the default state
- `.ui-state-hover`: CSS applies to clickable button-like elements when the mouse is hovering over it
- `.ui-state-focus`: CSS class to represent keyboard focus on clickable elements.
- `.ui-state-active`: CSS classes for a clickable element when it is selected (or mouse down)

Interaction cues are indications of the status of the element. Some of them are as follows:

- `.ui-state-disabled`: This will disable elements.
- `.ui-state-highlight`: This is used to highlight elements.
- `.ui-state-error`: CSS class to be applied to error messaging container elements.
- `.ui-icon` (icon related CSS classes): This base class is applied to an icon element by setting the dimensions of a 16 px square box. It hides the inner text and the background image applied to the content state image sprite.

Going beyond the standard PrimeFaces theme

The PrimeFaces theme gallery already provides more than 30 built-in themes if you want to choose the right theme for your applications. The theme gallery also includes other component library-specific themes, which are useful in migration.

For example, if you are using **Apache Trinidad** or **JBOSS RichFaces**, then the PrimeFaces theme gallery already contains Trinidad's **Casablanca** and RichFaces' **BlueSky** theme so that you can make PrimeFaces look like the Trinidad or RichFaces components during migration.

However, you will encounter many situations where none of the predefined PrimeFaces themes exactly fit your needs. In these cases, you can customize your own theme. We shouldn't start creating the theme from scratch. But first, you have to select a theme that is close to what you need and then tweak the theme as per your requirements using the ThemeRoller tool (Fore more information about ThemeRoller, visit http://jqueryui.com/themeroller/).

We have already discussed how to create custom themes for desktop and mobile applications in the previous chapters.

Override PrimeFaces CSS classes

You might frequently want to override the predefined PrimeFaces styles with customized values. Just changing the default values of the PrimeFaces CSS classes won't affect a web page.

You can override the CSS styles in the following two ways:

1. This is the simplest solution. Add an important keyword to the CSS properties in order to override the CSS styles, as follows:

```
.ui-message-info, .ui-message-error, .ui-message-warn, .ui-
  message-fatal {
  border: 1px solid;;
  margin: 0px 5px;
  padding:2px 5px;
}
```

Let's override the CSS properties such border, margin, and padding with
!important, as follows:

```
.ui-message-info, .ui-message-error, .ui-message-warn, .ui-
  message-fatal {
  border: 0!important;
  margin: 0!important;
  padding: 0!important;
}
```

All the preceding CSS properties being reset to zero results in message boxes
without dimension styles.

2. Resource ordering in PrimeFaces is the official way of overriding PrimeFaces
   styles. Have a look at http://blog.primefaces.org/?p=1433, a blog post,
   for more details about the resource ordering feature.

   In this case, you need to declare custom style sheets in the last facet after the
   head section, as follows:

```
<h:head>
  <!-- load other css, js and resources -->
</h:head>
<h:body>
<f:facet name="last">
  <h:outputStylesheet library="default" name="css/custom.css" />
</f:facet>
```

Override specific component CSS styles

If you want to change the style of a particular component instead of all the
components of a similar type, then you can add name spacing for the styles. In this
case, we can append the custom CSS class name for the built-in CSS classname and
use the custom CSS class for the component styleClass property.

Let's override the dialog component titlebar CSS properties, as follows:

```
.ui-dialog-titlebar {
  // CSS properties
}
Or
.ui-dialog-titlebar.ui-widget-header {
  // CSS properties
}
```

The preceding CSS properties will be reflected across all the components.

To apply CSS to a particular dialog component, you first need to add a custom CSS class for the built-in PrimeFaces styles, as follows:

```
.custom .ui-dialog-titlebar {
//CSS properties
}
```

Then, you just need to add a CSS class name to the dialog component, as follows:

```
<p:dialogstyleClass="custom">
..
</p:dialog>
```

So with the help of CSS class namespacing feature, you can make changes to specific components instead of adding to all the components.

Preview the theme styles before going to use

The main style classes of the PrimeFaces theme and the container or placeholder styles of each element are described well and clearly mentioned in the official documentation (the user guide). But it is difficult to demonstrate all the minor style classes, and they may not be available in any documentation section.

In this case, grab the theme.css from the theme jar and open it in CSS style editors such as **TopStyle** (http://topstyle4.com/) and **StyleMaster** (http://westciv.com/tools/) to preview the element style.

Considerations for mobile applications

As for best practices in PrimeFaces web applications, there are best practices that you need to follow in mobile applications as well. The real estate is the chief aspect that separates web and mobile applications when designing.

The following are some important notes that you need to remember before you start designing a mobile application:

- Maintain a good contrast between different swatch colors that are used for each mobile component.

- Keep the Rich UI forms simple and minimal. It is good practice to design a form with the fewest fields to retrieve data. Usually, these forms should be prefilled to reduce errors that may happen when typing on small touchscreens or virtual keyboards.

For example, use visual calendars instead of typing dates manually in the inputs.

- Keep simple menus and navigation styles. Desktop sites display big a menu bar at the top of the screen, whereas it eats up space if you use it. In this case, make a drop-down accordion or icon at the top-left or top-right of the mobile's screen.

- Use fluid layouts in your mobile pages. Many mobile devices means many different dimensions. You shouldn't design for one particular dimension (such as 400 px width). The page should work on different common device widths. In this case, we should use flexible layouts, such as fluid layouts.

- Drop the usage of images wherever possible. The performance of a mobile site depends on the speed and size of the site. So, if you are trying to use images for gradients, shadows, fancy text as images, and so on, then replace them with CSS effects in your design to minimize the footprint and page load time.

Busy UI versus data-dominated UI

This is wholly dependent on the type of web app that you are developing, but the type of web app that is best suited for the JSF framework tends to be data-dominated. Normally, in the busy UI type of applications, users have to perform multiple interactive actions and immediate dynamic changes in the frontend, which makes the user interface busy all the time. The user interface became too busy with JS, DOM operations, and AJAX requests along with plain HTTP requests. It is recommended that you use busy indicators after an action is performed and waiting for the result to get the data from the server. Making the UI too busy confuses the user and browsers will blow down after some time. You can also block the UI with the `blockUI` component from PrimeFaces in order to stop duplicate or multiple requests at a time. This approach is mainly used to create fancy applications.

Big applications mostly carry a lot of data and the JSF framework eyes on it by designing several data container components. The PrimeFaces UI component set especially provides a group of data-oriented components. You need to select the right data container with the required features. Considering this fact, the standard JSF or its component UI libraries have a special focus on data components.

Whatever the approach is, make sure that the final design is simple and easy to use.

Feedback from potential users

The website that you created either helps or harms your company or customer in all sorts of ways. Unfortunately, it can be really difficult to measure customer intent and gauge how well your website is performing unless you really talk to consumers about their experience. Also, it is good practice to get an overall user experience from the current web trends.

An online website feedback survey will be helpful in this case. From a developer's point of view, the PrimeFaces community forum (to have a look at this forum, visit `http://forum.primefaces.org/viewforum.php?f=3`) is also a good place to discuss how to create a better design. Users usually give feedback about what's missing in the design and what needs to be removed. Then, after receiving the feedback, you can redesign your website with the required theme changes according to customer requirements.

In this way, you can design a user interface that is commonly used and expected by many users.

Miscellaneous best practices

Some of the miscellaneous best practices that you should follow and which are not covered in the preceding sections are as follows:

- Maintain consistency across all pages. Things that perform similar functions should look and behave in similar ways
- Navigational elements should not dominate and should be as simple as possible for ease of use
- Make sure that the user is getting enough feedback when an operation is running (if it takes a significant amount of time) and whether it was successful or not

So, if you follow all the aforementioned best practices, then it is easy to create an awesome and unified look and feel and responsive applications during the design stage.

Summary

In this chapter, we explored the web WAI for good web design, best practices in the usage of colors, icon sets, and background and foreground colors. We had a look at how fonts make the text stand out in a website and the difference between rich Internet applications and desktop applications in the current era. We also learned the importance of feedback from potential users. We also learned the difference between busy UIs and the data-dominated approach. We had a look at the guidelines on functions per page, the components that you are going to use, how to override common CSS styles and specific styles by going beyond the standard PrimeFaces themes, the considerations for mobile, and a few other miscellaneous best practices.

In the next chapter, we are going to discuss about the premium PrimeFaces themes and layouts and features. We will study various premium distributions in depth and learn what latest technologies are used. We will also look at the party converter tools that are used to convert ThemeRoller themes to PrimeFaces-compatible themes.

11
Premium Themes and Layouts, and Third-party Converter Tools

In this chapter, we will look at premium themes and layouts apart from the regular community or free themes. After that, we will have a look at the setup and installation of premium themes. You'll learn how to easily customize CSS styles using the most popular CSS preprocessor called **Less** technology in premium themes and layouts. We'll study the support of the brand-new **Google Material Design** language. At the end, there's a brief coverage of themes and layouts features one by one.

We will also look at third-party converter tools to convert the ThemeRoller themes to PrimeFaces-compatible theme JAR files.

In this chapter, we will cover the following topics:

- Introducing premium themes and layouts
- Setup and installing premium themes
- Using CSS Less support to customize CSS styles easily
- Brand-new themes based on the Google Material Design language
- A brief coverage of the features provided by different premium themes and layouts
- Third-party theme converters

Introducing premium themes and layouts

In the previous chapters, we had a look at how to use predefined or built-in PrimeFaces themes and then create custom themes using jQuery ThemeRoller according to the required skinning. Later, the PrimeFaces team thought about creating advanced themes apart from the regular ThemeRoller ones. The `aristo` theme looks more advanced than any other community theme available because it has been developed by using the Photoshop technology. Therefore, the PrimeFaces team decided to develop all the **Elite** (a new commercial business model) themes in Photoshop.

In these Elite themes' development, the PrimeFaces team initially introduced the **MetroUI** theme, which was inspired by the Windows 8 Metro user interface. This MetroUI theme is well-designed in Photoshop for a better look and feel, and it can be subscribed for both Elite and **PRO** user licenses. But there were no new Elite themes developed after this first theme.

MetroUI is made available to the Elite subscribers through http://www.primefaces.org/elite/, the Elite portal.

The look and feel of MetroUI on various components will be as follows:

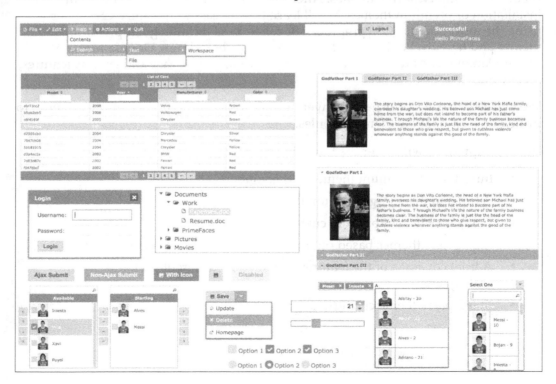

Later, PrimeFaces started premium themes and layouts with another new business or license model. Each premium artifact contains two main resources—layout and theme.

The **layout** is a responsive template that looks amazing. It comes with a set of XHTML files, including dashboard, login, error, 404 (or page not found), and empty-content, along with an icons pack and images to kick-start an application easily. It saves a lot of effort and time during development. All of these template pages and styles can be used as production ready.

The common features of each layout are as follows:

- A layout is created as a responsive layout with a clean, powerful, and ready-to-use design that is optimized for mobile devices as well.
- It is developed by modern technologies such as HTML5 and CSS3 with fallback for legacy browsers.
- It supports cross-browser compatibility and works smoothly on Google Chrome, Mozilla Firefox, Safari, Opera, Internet Explorer 9, and more.
- It supports modern fonts with the help of the Font Awesome font pack, **Fontello** icon fonts, material font packs, and custom fonts for sharp-looking fonts.
- Each layout comes with its own theme, which gives all the components a unified look and feel. This makes a theme compatible with the layout design in a proper way.
- It creates a pixel-perfect design with well-tested and production-ready layouts.

Each layout offers a compatible theme with the same design. You can also use these standalone themes without layouts, but it is recommended to use the theme of a layout for a unified look and consistent design in an application.

The following premium themes and layouts were introduced by the PrimeFaces team one by one after regular intervals:

- **Sentinel**
- **Spark**
- **Ronin**
- **Rio**
- **Modena**

After the initial releases of the aforementioned premium artifacts, there will be regular new releases with performance improvements and bug fixes.

The PrimeFaces team also planned below two new Premium themes and layouts with attractive features in the upcoming releases:

- Adamantium
- Volt

Setting up and installing premium themes

The setup and installation of premium themes and layouts is quite easy, and this process is the same for every premium distribution.

The setup and installation of a premium theme is similar to that of any other community theme. You just need to set the primefaces.THEME context param to the sentinel, spark, ronin, rio, or modena theme.

The setup and installation of a premium layout requires a step-by-step process, which is explained as follows:

- Each layout provides a main template.xhtml and additional layoutmenu. xhtml (the leftmenu.xhtml file for sentinel and topbar.xhtml for the base layout). You need to copy and place these three files under the WEB-INF folder of your project.

- To kick-start a page from scratch, use a layout provided by a sample empty-page.xhtml page (by using the main template.xhtml file) to define custom content, where *content* is the main ui:define placeholder.

- Each layout contains resources such as CSS, JavaScript, images, and font files that are located inside the resources/sentinel-layout folder. Copy the entire sentinel-layout folder to the %WEB-APP-FOLDER%/resources path. Now, the final path will be %WEB-APP-FOLDER%/resources/sentinel-layout.

You can further check an online demo application on the PrimeFaces site or a Maven project of a demo application as a reference.

Using CSS Less support to customize CSS styles easily

In recent years, CSS has matured into a very powerful web technology that can be used to style web pages. Now, it is possible to create an almost full-blown website in CSS with minimal usage of images. But while developing big websites, CSS style sheets are longer, harder to manage, and more complex to create. Due to this reason, many dynamic style sheet languages started and evolved. These languages help you write CSS rules using a more flexible, powerful language that is interpreted as regular CSS in web browsers. One of the many dynamic style sheet languages is **Less**, a popular CSS preprocessor that can be used to streamline CSS code, thus saving time and effort.

Less is a programmable style sheet language that extends the CSS language by combining programming concepts or features such as variables, mixins, functions, operations, and many other techniques that make CSS more maintainable, themeable, and extendable.

You can visit `http://lesscss.org/`, the officiate site of Less, for more information.

At the time of writing this book, the latest version of the Less JavaScript library is 1.2.1. The setup and configuration of Less is quite easy. Once the library is downloaded from the official website, it needs to be placed under the web project folder.

After that, add the link to the HTML document, as follows:

```
<script src="less-1.2.1.min.js" type="text/javascript"></script>
```

Premium themes and layouts are shipped with `less.js` configured in their web pages. Therefore, separate or additional configurations are not required.

Let's look at some of the common features of Less CSS in detail:

- The `variables` feature is used to control commonly used variables in a single location. For example, the following standard CSS uses the same color across all CSS classes:
  ```
  a, .link { color: #000080; }
  widget { color: #ffffff; background: #000080; }
  ```

In Less, you can reuse variables across a style sheet a number of times by just declaring them once. The preceding vanilla CSS can be rewritten as follows:

```
// Variables
@link-color: #000080; // sea blue

// Usage
a,
.link {
  color: @link-color;
}

.widget {
  color: #ffffff;
  background: @link-color;
}
```

- The mixins feature allows you to mix a bunch of properties from one rule-set into another rule-set. Let's create a .bordered class with the top and bottom borders in CSS, as follows:

```
.bordered {
  border-top: dotted 1px black;
  border-bottom: solid 2px black;
}
```

With the help of mixins, the above CSS class can be included in other rule-sets as follows:

```
#panel a {
  color: #111;
  .bordered;
}

.grid a {
  color: red;
  .bordered;
}
```

We can also use #ids as a mixin (not only as a class).

- Less provides some built-in functions, which transform colors, manipulate strings, and perform math calculations. For example, in the preceding code snippets, the percentage function is used to convert the width value to percentage, the saturate function is used to increase the base color by a specific percentage, and so on:

```
@base: #f04615;
@width: 0.5;

.class {
  width: percentage(@width); // converts 0.5 to`50%`
  color: saturate(@base, 5%); // increase the saturation of
  a base color by 5%
}
```

- The operations feature allows you to manipulate numbers, colors, variables, and so on. The following operations are as simple as normal math:

```
@base: 5%;
@filler: @base * 2;
@other: @base + @filler;
color: #888 / 4;
background-color: @base-color + #111;
height: 100% / 2 + @filler;
```

- Importing feature is similar to importing files in programming languages. You can import the .less files, which contain all the variables, as follows:

```
@import "library"; // library.less
@import "typo.css";
```

  As observed from the preceding code snippet, the extension is optional for the .less files.

Apart from the aforementioned concepts, there are many other useful programming techniques that help you easily customize colors, font sizes, borders, transitions, and other effects.

The latest premium themes and layouts, such as Modena and Rio distributions, use the Less technology. The Less files of the layout are located in the layout folder of the layout ZIP file, and the Less files of the theme are located in the theme folder of the theme JAR file. The major {layoutname} -layout and theme.css files can be customized using CSS Less. Both the layout and theme Less files contain their respective variable files that define the text color, background color, foreground color, border color, font size of elements, and so on. These variables will be reused in the main layout and the theme Less files.

For example, the font size of text in the top menu is declared in the variables file and used in the layout file, as follows:

```
@body-bg-color: #F5F5F5;
body{margin:0px; height:100%; width:100%; background-color:@body-
  bg-color; font-family:'robotolight';}
```

The Modena Less files such as `modena-layout.less` and `theme.less`, import `layout-variables.less` and `theme-variables.less` files, as follows:

```
@import "../variables/layout-variables.less";
@import "../variables/theme-variables.less";
```

The Less files are compiled in the standard CSS code files with the help of the **lessc** compiler. This compiler will convert the `{layoutname}-layout` and `theme.less` files into their respective CSS files.

Brand new themes based on Google Material Design language

Material design is a design language developed by Google. It is a comprehensive guide for visual, motion, and interactive design across various platforms and devices. It makes liberal use of grid-based layouts, responsive animations, transitions and effects, padding and depth effects such as lighting and shadow, and so on.

Initially, it was introduced by Google at the **Google I/O 2014 conference**. It was implemented for the first time in the Android Lollipop 5.0 release. It has been used in Google apps such as Gmail, YouTube, Inbox, Google Drive, Google Docs, and so on. **Material Design Lite** (MDL), **Polymer**, and **Angular Material** projects also provide official implementations. The PrimeFaces premium packages don't use any of these external libraries, but instead follow the material design specifications.

The latest releases of Modena and Rio introduced material font icons. The usage is quite simple; you just have to add the icon name and other skinning CSS classes, as follows:

```
<i class="icon-cloud_done Fs100 Red"></i>
```

The icon will be displayed with the `Fs100 Red` custom style, as follows:

The different color schemes of layout are also created based on material design. Apart from that, grid layouts, cards, responsive animations/transitions, and effects (such as the ripple effect) are inspired by the Google Material Design specification and guidelines. PrimeFaces doesn't use an external JS library implementation of the Google Material Design language, but it just follows the specification guidelines.

A brief coverage of different premium themes and layouts features

The PrimeFaces team planned to release premium themes and layouts on a periodic basis, which are created based on the latest web technologies. These themes and layouts are designed in such a way that they are compatible with both desktop and mobile platforms.

Let's list some of the common features observed in the preceding themes and layouts. In this section, we used Modena screenshots for demonstration purposes:

- All the premium theme distributions provide menus as a multilevel menu positioned to the left of the screen. It is just like the PrimeFaces menu component, but it is optimized with the latest premium CSS features. This menu is responsive, and it adjusts according to the screen width automatically. Since this component is available in the theme JAR file, it is mandatory to have the theme in the class path. This menu is stateFUL by default. Therefore, in order to work with the state-saving feature, you are required to provide explicit IDs for submenus and menu items. You can also clear the state by calling the `{themename}.clearMenuState()` JavaScript method.

The Modena menu component with a responsive design and effects will be as follows:

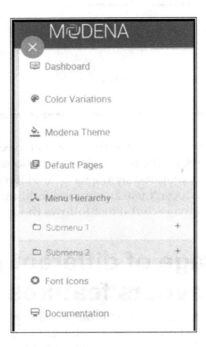

- Each premium theme and layout provides default pages, such as an empty page, a login page, an error page, a 404 page, and an access denied page, for quick and rapid development of applications. They will also provide a dashboard and a list of components supported by the theme and font icons. Remember that all of them support the Font Awesome icons, whereas the latest versions of Modena and Rio support Google Material Design fonts as well.

The login page with the commonly used HTML elements is shown in the following screenshot:

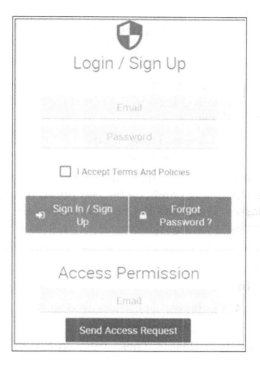

- The following core layout CSS classes are used to create responsive grid layouts and skinning and structural CSS styles:

    ○ **The Responsive Mode**: This makes elements more responsive by using media queries. The possible values for this case are `Responsive`, `Responsive50`, `Responsive100`, and so on.

    ○ **ContainerX**: This is used as part of grid layouts, where *X* represents the width of the cell. You can also add a responsive style class to make it responsive. For example, some of the possible values are `Container5`, `Container10`, `Container20`, and so on. Since these `container` classes float, a `container` class should be the parent if you need to clear the floats:

    ```
    .Container5{ width:5%; float:left;}
    .Container10{ width:10%; float:left;}
    .Container20{ width:20%; float:left;}
    ```

- **Text color CSS classes**: These are used to apply various predefined selected colors to the text. For example, `grayblue`, `red`, and `navyblue`.

- **Background color CSS classes**: These are used to paint the selected color on elements' backgrounds. For example, `grayblue`, `redback`, and `navyblueback`.

- **Top border coloring CSS classes**: These are used to determine the upper limit with color and the pixels that border on shadow boxes or any other elements.

- **Section CSS classes**: These are used to unselect a particular text. A possible CSS class name is `Unselectable`.

- **Visibilities, floating and width settings**: These are based on device screen sizes and can be configured by using their respective CSS classes. The possible CSS class names are `ShowOnMobile`, `ShowOnDesktop`, `FloatNoneOnMobile`, and `WidAutoOnMobile`.

- **Positioning CSS classes**: These are used to position elements relative to other elements.

- **Underline CSS class**: This is used to define the text which is below.

- **Floating CSS classes**: These are used to float the element either to the left or right, or no direction.

- **Overflow CSS classes**: These are used to define the overflow properties of an element's content.

- **EmptyBoxes CSS classes**: These are used to define specific pixels of empty spaces between text content.

- **Opacity CSS classes**: These define element transparency up to a specified value.

- **WidX CSS classes**: These define the element data width with a specified percentage value.

- **TextAligning CSS classes**: These are used to align text to the left or right or in the center.

- **BoxSizing CSS classes**: These are used to define box sizes based on the content, border, padding, margin, and so on.

- **FontSize CSS classes**: These define a specific font size for elements in pixels.

- **Font weight CSS classes**: These are used to define the font weight for characters.

- ○ **Less curve CSS class**: This is used to reduce the border radius of child elements.

- ○ **Transition timings CSS classes**: These define CSS3 transitions with a specified duration.

- ○ **The CSS classes that are used to display the elements in a specific element format**: The possible CSS class names are `DispBlock`, `DispNone`, `DispTable`, `DispInlBlock`, and `DispTableCell`.

 Note that detailed coverage of the aforementioned core CSS classes with examples is available in each premium distribution's documentation section.

Some of the premium distributions that also support layout-specific features are as follows:

- The latest premium distributions such as Modena and Rio use the Less technology in their layout and theme CSS files. This feature is not supported in the previous or older premium distributions.

- Modena supports five color alternatives for the top bar and body background in terms of the background image (`Blue`, `Gray`, `Red`, `Indigo`, and `Cyan`). It has to be defined for `h:body styleClass` (for example, `styleClass="BlueModena Geometry"`). On the other hand, the Spark layout provides four color alternatives — `green`, `blue`, `orange`, and `red`.

- The Modena and Rio distributions support some of the layout CSS classes on cards for grouping, text colors, background colors, borders, separators, effects, the Roboto font, and so on.

The card component for grouping is used with the footer area at the bottom of card elements, as follows:

In the preceding case, we should add the `CardFooter` CSS class for footer display, whereas the `CardTopic` and `Card` CSS classes are also used for the top area and the main container.

There is already a demo application created for each of them along with a proper documentation section. The usage is well explained with examples to cover all scenarios. For example, you can view the demo and documentation by visiting `http://primefaces.org/modena/`, the Modena site.

Third-party theme converters

As you already know, the ThemeRoller themes can't be used directly on the PrimeFaces components. They need to be modified as it suits the PrimeFaces infrastructure. Once you download the custom themes from the ThemeRoller tool, you need to perform the following steps:

1. On `http://jqueryui.com/download/`, the download page of the ThemeRoller site, you need to uncheck the **Toggle All** option in order to make a theme file contain only skinning styles.

2. Rename the `jquery-ui-theme.css` file to the `theme.css` file and then copy the `images` folder.

3. Convert the `images` reference in the `theme.css` file to an expression that JSF can understand. For example, the `image` reference in `theme.css` is as follows:

   ```
   url("images/ui-bg_flat_30_cccccc_40x100.png")
   ```

   The preceding reference should be modified as follows:

   ```
   url("#{resource['primefaces-themename:images/ui-
     bg_flat_30_cccccc_40x100.png']}")
   ```

4. After doing this, create a JAR file with the following folder structure:

   ```
   - jar
     -META-INF
       - resources
         - primefaces-themename
           - theme.css
           - images
   ```

5. Now, apply theme JAR, which follows the PrimeFaces theme convention and folder structure, to the class path of your project.

Finally, our theme is applied to the PrimeFaces components.

The preceding process needs to be done manually for each theme, and it is a time-consuming process. To overcome this process, some third-party converters came into the picture, which makes the conversion of the ThemeRoller themes to PrimeFaces-compatible themes very easy and saves a lot of effort of developers.

Initially, the first third-party converter tool authored by Maxim Maximchuk was titled the **PrimeFaces theme converter**. It is a small and efficient utility that will make it possible to transform the ThemeRoller themes to the PrimeFaces themes. It is a handy and easy-to-use application available in the ZIP format. You can download the application from `http://www.softpedia.com/get/Programming/Other-Programming-Files/Primefaces-theme-converter.shtml`, the official site's download section.

Unzip the `ptc.1.0.zip` file and click on the `run_gui.bat` file to run the application.

From the GUI, browse the ThemeRoller theme that you want to convert, choose a custom name, and click on the **Create theme** button:

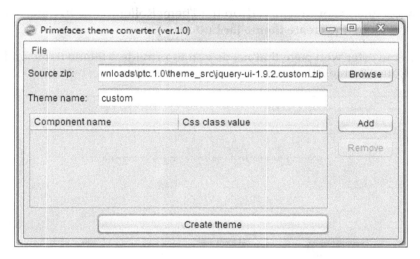

The application creates a `theme-out` folder inside the `application` folder, where it stores the converted PrimeFaces `custom.jar` theme. Now, the newly created theme can be placed in the class path of your project to apply the skinning on the PrimeFaces components.

Later, another third-party converter was introduced. It was titled **ThemeRoller theme to PrimeFaces theme converter**. This converter is an online tool or application. The application itself is created with a PrimeFaces 4.0 library and built by OSnode. The official site can be viewed by visiting `https://themeroller.osnode.com/themeroller/index.xhtml`.

The step-by-step procedure that is required to create the PrimeFaces theme JAR file is as follows:

1. Create a custom theme from the ThemeRoller website. Note that the supported ThemeRoller versions are 1.11.4, 1.11.3, 1.11.2, 1.11.1, 1.10.4, and 1.9.2.

2. Uncheck the component's **Toggle All** checkbox, leave the **Theme Folder Name** as `custom-theme`, and download the resulting ZIP file. Note that you must not change the name of the ThemeRoller ZIP file that you are uploading as it contains the version number.

3. Provide a theme name in the input box.

4. Choose the file or drag and drop the ThemeRoller theme in the ZIP format and click on the **create theme jar** button.

The online converter web page that needs you to provide a theme name and upload the ThemeRoller theme ZIP file is shown in the following screenshot:

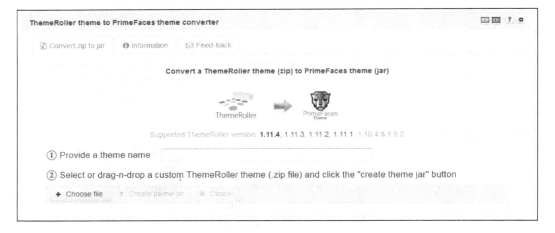

The PrimeFaces theme will be generated in a theme JAR file. Now, the theme JAR file is ready to use on the PrimeFaces project.

In this way, premium themes and layouts create the more advanced themes, whereas third-party theme converters reduce the manual effort of creating the PrimeFaces infrastructure or convention themes.

Summary

In this chapter, we explored premium themes and layouts, Less support for easy customization of CSS styles, Google Material Design in brand-new layouts and themes, the various features provided by different types of premium themes and layouts, and some third-party converters that are used to convert the ThemeRoller themes to the PrimeFaces-compatible theme JAR files.

After reading this book, you will be a professional designer or developer who can create PrimeFaces applications using various built-in and custom themes. You are familiar with the different ways that can be used to create a design with an awesome look and feel as per the modern trends and requirements. You also know how various latest web technologies and tools helps to create to optimized, flexible, and responsive applications. You can now create themes with best practices and apply them on desktop and mobile platforms.

The advanced premium themes and layouts keep on evolving and being released on a periodic basis with some common goals such as responsive design, grid layouts, effects, and production ready to use common web pages. Keep on eye for upcoming new premium themes and layouts in PrimeFaces blog!

We wish you all the best! We hope you have a good time developing PrimeFaces themeable projects!

Index

Symbols

Thank you for buying
PrimeFaces Theme Development

About Packt Publishing

Packt, pronounced 'packed', published its first book, *Mastering phpMyAdmin for Effective MySQL Management*, in April 2004, and subsequently continued to specialize in publishing highly focused books on specific technologies and solutions.

Our books and publications share the experiences of your fellow IT professionals in adapting and customizing today's systems, applications, and frameworks. Our solution-based books give you the knowledge and power to customize the software and technologies you're using to get the job done. Packt books are more specific and less general than the IT books you have seen in the past. Our unique business model allows us to bring you more focused information, giving you more of what you need to know, and less of what you don't.

Packt is a modern yet unique publishing company that focuses on producing quality, cutting-edge books for communities of developers, administrators, and newbies alike. For more information, please visit our website at www.packtpub.com.

About Packt Open Source

In 2010, Packt launched two new brands, Packt Open Source and Packt Enterprise, in order to continue its focus on specialization. This book is part of the Packt Open Source brand, home to books published on software built around open source licenses, and offering information to anybody from advanced developers to budding web designers. The Open Source brand also runs Packt's Open Source Royalty Scheme, by which Packt gives a royalty to each open source project about whose software a book is sold.

Writing for Packt

We welcome all inquiries from people who are interested in authoring. Book proposals should be sent to author@packtpub.com. If your book idea is still at an early stage and you would like to discuss it first before writing a formal book proposal, then please contact us; one of our commissioning editors will get in touch with you.

We're not just looking for published authors; if you have strong technical skills but no writing experience, our experienced editors can help you develop a writing career, or simply get some additional reward for your expertise.

PrimeFaces Cookbook
Second Edition
ISBN: 978-1-78439-342-7   Paperback: 412 pages

Over 100 practical recipes to learn PrimeFaces 5.x –
the most popular JSF component library on the planet

1. The updated second edition of the first
    PrimeFaces book ever released is brought
    to you straight from the horse's mouth, and
    focuses on practical implementations of the
    framework rather than theoretical ones.

2. With this book, you will get everything you
    need to know about PrimeFaces first-hand
    and will learn how to easily integrate and use
    PrimeFaces successfully with your JSF projects.

3. This book is written in a clear, comprehensible
    style and addresses a wide audience who set
    their scope on Java EE development.

PrimeFaces Blueprints
ISBN: 978-1-78398-322-3   Paperback: 310 pages

Create your very own portfolio of customized web
applications with PrimeFaces

1. Learn how to use the rich UI components
    of PrimeFaces.

2. Explore all the major features of PrimeFaces
    with real-world examples.

3. Step-by-step guide with precise explanations of
    code and functionalities.

Please check **www.PacktPub.com** for information on our titles

Learning PrimeFaces Extensions Development

ISBN: 978-1-78398-324-7   Paperback: 192 pages

Develop advanced frontend applications using PrimeFaces Extensions components and plugins

1. Learn how to utilize the enhanced Extensions' components in the existing or newly created PrimeFaces based applications.

2. Explore all the components major features with lots of example scenarios.

3. Features a systematic approach to teach a wide range of Extensions component features with the JobHub web application development.

Mastering PrimeFaces [Video]

ISBN: 978-1-78398-806-8   Duration: 5:04 hours

Master the PrimeFaces Component framework and quickly develop sophisticated web applications

1. Develop sophisticated user interfaces for your Java EE applications utilizing the Ajax core components.

2. Master the PrimeFaces powerful JSF component library to build your application.

3. Portray outstanding visual dashboards for your data.

Please check **www.PacktPub.com** for information on our titles

www.ingramcontent.com/pod-product-compliance
Lightning Source LLC
Chambersburg PA
CBHW060553060326
40690CB00017B/3693

* 9 7 8 1 7 8 3 9 8 8 6 8 6 *